TRANSFIGURED WORLD

TRANSFIGURED WORLD

Design, Theme and Symbol in Worship

By
Sister M. Laurentia Digges, C.S.J.

Illustrated by
Sister Charlotte Anne Carter, C.S.J.

AROUCA PRESS

Originally published by Farrar, Straus and Cudahy (New York) in 1957

Reprinted by Arouca Press 2021

All rights reserved:
No part of this book may be reproduced or transmitted,
in any form or by any means, without permission

ISBN: 978-1-989905-42-5 (pbk)
ISBN: 978-1-989905-43-2 (hardcover)

Arouca Press
PO Box 55003
Bridgeport PO
Waterloo, ON N2J3G0
Canada
www.aroucapress.com
Send inquiries to info@aroucapress.com

Nihil obstat
    John A. Goodwine, J.C.D.
    Censor Librorum

Imprimatur
    ✠ Francis Cardinal Spellman
    Archbishop of New York

The nihil obstat and imprimatur are official declarations that a book or pamphlet is free of doctrinal or moral error. No implication is contained therein that those who have granted the nihil obstat and the imprimatur agree with the contents, opinions or statements expressed.

For two Marys

The purpose of the Christian religion is to assimilate man to God through Christ . . . to bring us as transfigured Christians to the transfigured Christ.

This is accomplished through sacrifice and sacrament and prayer, that is, through the liturgy.

The idea of Christian transfiguration is the art-principle of the liturgy.

DOM HERWEGEN [1]

. . . Only by the form, the pattern,
Can words or music reach
The stillness.

T. S. ELIOT [2]

Contents

PREFACE		viii
INTRODUCTION		ix

FIRST PART

ONE	Of Four Things a Man Loves	3
TWO	Of Circles and the Design of the Liturgy	33
THREE	Of Transfiguration: the Theme of the Liturgy	45
FOUR	Of Symbols and the Four Elements	67

TRANSITION

FIVE	Of Christ the Center	81

SECOND PART

SIX	Of the Mass: First Circle	95
SEVEN	Of the Sacraments: Second Circle	139
EIGHT	Of the Office: Third Circle	177
NINE	Of the Year: Fourth Circle	203
APPENDIX I	Of the Illustrations	235
APPENDIX II	Of the Authors Quoted	237

Preface

TODAY THERE IS a growing eagerness to enter into a deeper knowledge of the Mass, the sacraments, and the whole life of the Church. Men welcome any illumination of these realities. Now one kind of insight which is particularly rewarding comes from a penetration of the actual words, gestures, and symbols used in worship. This book has been written for the general Catholic reader who desires such illumination.

Accordingly, in the book, the principal method has been to look quietly at the actual texts of the liturgy itself—the Mass, the sacraments, the office, and the year of grace. These have been given a central position, and on them have been focused some of the lights which art offers—for the primary function of art is to serve as an illumination, a revelation, an epiphany.

An attempt to name all the persons to whom I am indebted for material, assistance, and inspiration, would lead back farther than the memory can go. Special mention should be made of Dr. G. Giovannini, Professor of English Literature at Catholic University of America; Rev. Godfrey Deikmann, Editor of *Worship*, whose course on the Mass I attended in Washington; and Rev. Stephen Pearson, now of St. Paschal's College, Melbourne. Some of their ideas are here, but they have for the most part become so assimilated to my thinking, and so modified by my own reflections, that it has proved impossible to choose separate phrases and footnote them.

My thanks are also owing to my family and many friends who believed this book could be written, especially to those who read it in manuscript; to Sister Marie de Lourdes, C.S.J., first teacher of poetry; and to the Sisters of St. Joseph of Carondelet, the Community to which I have the good fortune to belong. To my colleagues at Mount St. Mary's College, Los Angeles, I owe a special debt. Without them there would have been no book.

Introduction

THE CHRISTIAN LIFE is a joyous life because God is not only the goal, he is also the way. "All the way to heaven is heaven," says St. Catherine of Siena, "for he said, 'I am the way.'" Therefore it is true to say that "God is our adventure," [3] and that every Christian has a vocation to joy.

Now in setting out on an adventure—an exploration—we know that both our learning and our delight are increased if someone is along to show us how to look. For to see relationships among things, to catch new insights into the beauty and meaning of things, deepens our enjoyment in every adventure. We are setting out to explore the world of worship which is called the liturgy: to discover some of its relationships to the world we see and hear and touch, to find out why it is a sublime work of art as well as a significant and transforming reality. In this exploration, there are certain things we do not wish to miss. To point out these significances and relationships is one aim of this book.

Perhaps someone has, one day, stood with you looking up at a wooded hillside, and told you to notice all the shades of green and textures of leaves and needles: acacia's chartreuse lace, dusty green pulp-thick olive leaves, peppers dangling indolent fronds, the lustrous near-blue of magnolia in deep shade. Forever after, you will have found a new delight in looking at trees.[4]

Again, think how your delight is deepened on a visit to an art gallery if you have a companion who knows about painting, and who says: Look at the way the light from the window is reflected on the floor; notice how this curve is balanced by that one; see, here the figures form a triangle.

The same thing holds good for adventures in amateur photography. You can learn how a scene is framed between a tree and a wall; you begin to catch contrasts of light and shade, to wonder if the glow of city lights at night could be caught with color film.

Such seeing of the qualities of unity cannot be done at a glance. Today we are in the habit of whizzing along in trains and cars so swiftly, seeing the passing world only as a blur, that our faculty of seeing things as wholes, and in all their sharp detail, has become blunted. We are more used to trying to count telephone poles as they whistle past, than we are likely to stop and admire the shape of a shadow that a cloud drops on a mountain.

For this reason, the poet (and painter and sculptor) tries to arrest us. He wants us to stop and look and listen. But sometimes, unless we know what to look and listen for, we are too impatient to stop at all. The same purpose is present in the shaping of the wonderful work of art which is the liturgy—that system of worship which God, in his Church, has given us for the praise of his glory.

The Church, too, wants us to stop and look and be enriched by the glories she presents for our contemplation. She wishes that by this penetration into God's mysteries we should be assimilated to Christ, and secondarily she wishes that all our powers may be unified through such quiet focusing of our gaze on the things of God.

When we dwell in this way on the beauties of the liturgy, we sometimes find new epiphanies—new revelations of God's glory—occuring. The exercise might be described this way: Your eyes and mind move by spurts along the words of the Mass, or the texts for the administration of the sacraments, or the year of grace. Your thoughts move, now swiftly, now halting for a moment, like the flame traveling down the wick of a fire-cracker. Then, just at the right moment, flame and powder make contact and the whole thing explodes into illumination.

This is one of the effects which Hopkins, the poet, said a poem should have. And the liturgy is a magnificent poem, though it is much more than this too. At other times, while we focus our powers intently in this way, we find that little explosions occur all the way down the text we are reading, the picture we are studying—little bursts of understanding light up our minds as we proceed.

Another enlightening thing which someone might say to us is this: Watch how the artist is true to his materials. This wood carving, for example, see how it tapers slimly upwards. Because it is wood, because it came from a tree, therefore it is shaped so. You know how a tree grows upward, and how its branches go out from the trunk—all with an ever-increasing slenderness. That is why the carving is slender.

Or again, look at this sandstone carving of St. Benedict. It is heavy and squat because the nature of sandstone is to cling to earth with immovable stability. This is particularly good material for St. Benedict, because his ideas were wise in the rhythms of earth, because his work took strong hold of natural things like the growing crops and the growing mind of man. He entered closely into the changing and returning seasons and days—and then, powerfully, he directed them all toward their transfiguration in God. For these reasons, this heavy sandstone statue of St. Benedict is true to its materials, and it is also true to its subject.

In somewhat the same way, we may say that God, the supreme artist, is true to his materials and to his subject. His materials in the liturgy are all the things of our world: the words and gestures of man, the earth and air and fire and water of material nature. His subject is his own divine life, his own glory made visible to us in the person of his divine and incarnate Son. And through our contact with his Son, by means of the liturgy (as well as in our individual faith and prayer and work), we are to be transfigured into his likeness—we are to be made a part of his living mystical body.

The aim of the book, then, in these more concrete terms, is to point out some of the ways in which God, the divine artist, uses his materials in order to effect his purpose which is the transfiguration of man. We shall see that he is true to his materials, actualizing their natural beauty in countless ways. And even more importantly, he invests the things of nature with supernatural meaning and power—a power which can "bring God within our reach" (as the Christmas Mass says). This is a power which not only brings God down to us, but also lifts man up to God—to a sharing in the very life of God.

That we may share in his divine life—this is God's great purpose in the liturgy. It is by this sharing that his glory is furthered and our happiness is brought about. Julian of Norwich,[5] a medieval mystic, has phrased this "urgency" of God's in memorable words. She says that there are "three kinds of longing in God: to teach us, to have us, to fulfill us."

Through the liturgy he does all three. *He teaches us* by leading us from the known to the unknown—by using our familiar material things to reveal his mysteries to us. *He has us*—for the whole end of the liturgy is to bring us to that union with him which is the fruit and end of all our life. And in thus bringing us into union with him, *he fulfills us*—for to find him is the deepest need of our being.

In order to deepen our insight into this transformation of man, in order to understand this transfiguration which is the art principle of the liturgy, we need to know some of the qualities which should be found: (a) in any good work of art; (b) in that divine art-work which is the liturgy. We shall, accordingly, discuss the four qualities of unity, variety, significance, and power, in the first chapter. The first two of these, and to some extent the third quality also, are requisites of art—of all kinds of art. The third and fourth relate more clearly to the supernatural purpose of the liturgy.

After these four are clearly seen, we shall next examine three cardinal principles which function in art—and function most admirably in God's masterpiece, the liturgy. These cardinal principles are: (1) structure, (2) theme, and (3) symbolism.

First there is structure itself—the way things are put together, the interrelationships among the different parts of the work. We might think of it, for example as the effect this bright splash of yellow will have on the surrounding colors in the picture, the change which comes to a high violin note because a cello moves along steadily beneath it, the impact which belongs to the end of a short story because all incidents have been dovetailed to its final revelation.

In our investigation of the liturgy's structure we shall find that it may be described as built on a system of four concentric circles, all dependent on Christ who is the center, and all modified by their relationship to him and to each other. For this reason, the second chapter will discuss the meaning and functions of this concentric structure.

The second principle to be discussed is theme. This might be defined as the repeated but varied statement of central meaning which permeates the whole work of art with significance. In the liturgy, this theme is one of transfiguration. The important statement which the liturgy makes is this—that through God's grace man, and even the things of the material world are transfigured. They are invested with glory. The meaning which the liturgy presents in a thousand different ways is this one of transfiguration. When we study it we find that the natural world is shown to us as possessed of new beauty. And we discover that its glorified elements mean one thing: man's transfiguration.

We find, besides, that the liturgy not only means transfiguration, it also makes it happen. It is, therefore, not only significant, but it is likewise in-formed with power. This power works to transfigure man into the likeness of Christ, through the use of natural instruments which are themselves transfigured for and through the process. All this is for one final end—the endowing of nature and of man with greater power to glorify God. The third chapter in this book is concerned with this theme of transfiguration and its operations in the liturgy.

Chapter four presents an explanation of the next principle which is symbolism. This is explored only in so far as it is necessary to our purpose in the book. The discussion is particularly concerned to point out various aspects of the four symbolic elements of earth, air, fire, and water: their meaning and related symbols, and their relevance to the transfigured world of worship.

These qualities of unity, variety, significance, and power, and these principles of circular structure, transfiguration theme, and elemental symbols are discussed in the first four chapters because they are interesting and valuable concepts in themselves and can add much delight to our lives. But more importantly, they are presented because an understanding of them illuminates the work of supernatural art which is the liturgy.

According to this way of looking at things we can see that the divine art of the liturgy illumines the world of nature, rendering visible to us new glory and new meaning in the things that make up our everyday world. Then further, the transfigured world of nature indicates for us, and serves as an instrument in the transfiguration of man.

Man's transfiguring begins with the new birth of baptism and continues through all of life. During life his efforts to serve God are unfailingly helped by the sacramental and sacrificial realities of the liturgy. And this great activity of

INTRODUCTION

glorification culminates in the utter fulfillment of man absorbed at last in the beatific vision of God, where he pours out his whole being in giving thanks for God's great glory. With these things the first half of the book is concerned.

Once having cleared up these preliminary notions, we shall be ready to contemplate the world of the liturgy itself. We shall see that the center of this whole world (and the center of the book) rests on Christ. He is the central figure in creation, the center Person in the mystery of the Godhead—"mid-numbered he in three of the thunder-throne," [6] as Hopkins says—and the central reality of all our worship of God. To this center, chapter five is devoted.

After this middle chapter, the second half of the book treats the four majestic circles which wheel around Christ the center. These are the Mass, the sacraments, the office in its various forms, and the seasons of the liturgical year. One chapter will be devoted to each of these, and in each we shall study the way the theme of transfiguration operates in and through the structure of the liturgical reality, and also the functioning of earth, air, fire, and water symbols and their relationship to the transfiguration of nature and of man.

These last, in ancient times, were thought to constitute the four ingredients from which everything in the universe was made. They therefore stand for the whole of creation. We know, moreover, that even today these four things are still most important in every man's life. Because of God's working in and through the four elements, they are useful to man on the purely natural level, but above all they are charged with meaning and effectiveness when he employs them for supernatural purposes. And htey appear, as we shall see, in each of the four circles which surround Christ the center.

In chapter six, which is next, we shall study the Mass as it moves in perpetually renewed offering to God, bringing the unchanged sacrifice of Calvary into our time and space so that we may make daily contact with redemption.

Then in chapter seven, we shall treat some aspects of the sacraments and sacramentals. They are pictured as the second circle in our design, just outside that of the Mass. These realities touch the circle of man's life at every point.

Next we shall discuss the third ring—the hours of each day as they are empowered to praise God, renew man, and reveal new beauty in nature by the Hours of the divine office and related prayers. Here it is well to remind ourselves that there are other cyclic patterns in the measurement of time, such as the moon's circle of the month, and the weekly return of the Sunday. But these are not so intricately wrought in the design of worship as the patterns of the day, man's lifetime, and the year. We shall, therefore, not discuss them at any length. Chapter eight, then, will be on the sacraments and related realities.

Finally in chapter nine we will concern ourselves with the circle of the litigurical year which by its constant renewal of Christ's mysteries brings us into ever deeper union with him. Such is the design: Christ as the point at the center, and four concentric circles in order around him.

After contemplating these tremendous realities, certain insights should have become our permanent possession—insights about such things as the admirable unity traceable in the four great circles of the liturgy, and their relationship to Christ who is the point at the center of it all. And we will have new ideas about such things as the way God uses our well loved and familiar earth and air, fire and water, seasons and gestures and words. We shall see him showing us beauties in them which we never before suspected, and empowering them with ability to transfigure men into the image of Christ.

FIRST PART

CHAPTER ONE

Of Four Things a Man Loves

> ... a world in which ... God is
> anything but a sleeping partner.
>
> CHRISTOPHER FRY [7]

SINCE WE ARE HUMAN BEINGS and not disembodied spirits, since we shall never be angels, since "man's spirit will be flesh-bound when found at best" [8]—therefore we are delighted when we find that not only earthly enjoyment, but even heavenly holiness is enriched by the realities of the material world, by the earth, and air, and fire, and water around us.

The first effect of such an appreciation of the art qualities of the liturgy is a new insight into the beauty even of the natural world. Happily for us, God, in shaping his art-work, was aware of our tendency to be enthralled by means as well as oriented towards ends.

He therefore laid much stress on our material world in his sacramental and sacrificial design of the liturgy. And in doing this he planned that Mother Church should be wonderfully earthly. This earthliness, in its best sense, shapes and informs God's own plan for his worship and our sacramental union with him. As we proceed we shall see how God the artist is always true to his materials.

All this being so, is it not possible that God wills us to

enjoy and reverence this world which he has so "wonderfully created and still more wonderfully renewed" (to use the words of the Mass which refer to redeemed human nature)? He has created it with inexhaustible natural variety, and renewed it still more wonderfully by designing it into beauty and using it for his own supernatural purposes.

Let us allow our minds to circle around these ideas. For the moment we will think about people as if they were all divided into two classes: tight-rope walkers, and Sunday afternoon strollers—people who are not, or try not to be, interested in this passing world, and people who, while loving God, find themselves also rejoicing in the things he has made. Someone has characterized these two modes of seeking God as the way of negation and the way of affirmation. Both are good. In this book, however, we are going to be most interested in the way of affirmation. Let us, however, look more closely at each of these ways.

Some people, for example, like men balanced on a tight-rope, walk straight across the world. They leave foot prints in a line and waste no movements as they strike out toward their goal. Like tight-rope walkers, they are concerned only with balance, with eliminating anything which could upset their hard-held equilibrium. They look neither to right nor left; their concern is never with means. Rather they fix their eyes on the goal alone.

Here is a poem which, even by its architecture, its structural lines, pictures such a tensity of balance. It suggests a hard-won equilibrium—a balance which the smallest addition on one side or the other would upset. (This, and not mere affectation, is the reason for the omission of the heavy capital letters. They would weigh the poem down on one side.)

The thought in the poem is that tight-rope walkers, in order to remain in perfect balance (notice the central placement of the key word, *balance*), in order to come safely to their goal, must ignore both the lure of earth and the lion of danger under the rope. They must be blind to everything on their way, and focus solely on the steady platform ahead. Here is the poem [9]:

tight-rope

feet feel secure, know where they're due
the eye is the mischief, always
turning, searching outward:
would ruin me
balance
preserved by
the toes; ignore
the dust and gravity's pull.
(eye travels faster to safety than limb.)

rope-walk is over a jealous lion.
the trick is to keep the eye fixed:
feet will provide themselves.

This effort to preserve equilibrium, to pivot on nothing but one's own weight, is a challenge, and so has its own attractions. But tight-rope walking at its best is a tense and lonely journey, and can be persevered in only by strenuous effort. It is true, of course, that sometimes we must be tight-rope walkers, giving no glance to our feet, but watching the goal unwaveringly. In this way we learn not to snatch at things, nor to cling to them.

On the other hand, we know that it is possible and good to live in such a way that we share God's delight in his own creation. In the beginning he made it all, and then looking around, he "saw it and found it good."

This expression of God's pleasure in his creation occurs six times in the first chapter of Genesis. And the last time it is intensified: "And God saw all that he had made, and found it very good" (Gen. 1:31).[10]

His joy in the things he has made and his watchful care for all never wavers, for he is "that Father from whom all fatherhood in heaven and on earth takes its title" (Eph. 3:15). But God is concerned with the world in other ways too. He is not only Creator and Father.

We know that God the Son came into the world, for "the Word was made flesh and came to dwell among us" (John 1:14). He shared our world with us. Like us, he walked on earth and ate its fruit; he breathed in its air, and warmed himself at fires; he found cool refreshment in water. We know that he felt the texture of bread and experienced the way it becomes sweet in the mouth. He felt the weight of clothes as they hung from his shoulders. He suffered our dust, challenged the power of storms, and found haven in the loneliness of our mountains.

Finally, not only the Father and the Son, but even the Holy Spirit, in his own special way has become involved (to speak in human fashion of ineffable things) with our lowly materiality. For out of it he shapes his wonderful design of sacrament and sacrifice.

It is no wonder that Christopher Fry, the modern British playwright, says that this "is a world in which we are all poised on the edge of eternity, a world which has deeps and shadows of mystery, in which God is anything but a sleeping partner."

People who stop to reverence the material world, know that God is close to creation. They can hear him as he walks "on the wings of the wind" (Ps. 103), and they sense his swift rejoicing. He is so near to everything they see and taste and touch that they know he means it literally when he says, not "I will *show* you the way," but "I *am* the way." He not only walks our roads with us, but he is the very road we walk. He himself is our adventure. And this is especially true when we cultivate an attitude of leisurely admiration—when we become at times "Sunday afternoon strollers."

It is good sometimes to circle across paths and come back to them, to gather golden weeds on one side and pine cones on the other. It can be a praise of God when we stand and stare at hollyhocks ragged against a gray fence, or when we halt to hear a crow's harsh exclamation as he swoops against storm clouds. And if God has so wonderfully made these natural things, how much more wonderfully he has shaped the sacramental world which uses natural things for supernatural ends.

God is our way because, as we have said, he is involved with it all—as Father, as Word made flesh, as activating Spirit. He works continually in it, like the master artist he is, shaping material and spiritual realities into the beauty of pattern and design. In this way he transforms all things. He transfigures man by setting alight in him the likeness of Christ. He transmutes the created world—changing its common materials into the glow of revelation, empowering creatures to glorify God, and to become instruments to transmit grace from God to man.

To live in this awareness is to discover the delightful individuality in things and the great unity among things—a unity composed of what Chesterton might have called the "wildest variety." When we realize this variety and this unity, and when, further, we discover in creation an underlying significance and an awe-inspiring power, then we have truly discovered that God is our adventure.

We might look at these ideas in another fashion and say that by the fact of God's becoming our *way* we are freed from all our loneliness. This freedom brings such joy that the water of our ordinary world is changed into an exhilarating wine. God has looked at us, we might say, and thought (in words once used by his mother): "They have no wine" (John 2:4). It is as if he were thinking: Their joy is not full. But I am come that their joy may be full. The wedding feast of their life which is to be lived with me has something lacking to it, and therefore I will change the water of their natural life into the wine of another life—one filled with supernatural joy. This wine will vivify their every day and vitalize all their actions.

Since, therefore, God is "anything but a sleeping partner," our exploration of reality becomes a never-ending adventure. Realizing this, we might say with Alice Meynell, the English poet,[11]

> Thou art the Way.
> Hadst Thou been nothing but the goal,
>   I cannot say
> If Thou hadst ever met my soul.

The poet means that no matter how wonderful the final vision of God (the goal) is to be, we cannot live on anticipation alone. We human beings are immersed, willy nilly, in things of space and time. God as the goal of the journey, might never see our wayfaring soul, if he were only the end and reward and nothing else. We know this well, and so we continue:

> I cannot see—
> I, child of process—if there lies
>   An end for me,
> Full of repose, full of replies.

Just because we are "children of process," engrossed with ways and means, we have but faint appreciation for far off goals. But the poem, at the end, says triumphantly that all is well. God is not only the goal. He is also the way:

> Access, Approach, art Thou—
> Time, Way, and Wayfarer.

Here again we catch the echo of St. Catherine's thought: "All the way to heaven is heaven, for he said, 'I am the way.'" God *is* our adventure.

Furthermore, it is especially when we contemplate the use that God makes of material things in the liturgy, that we feel the world is "touched by deeps and shadows of mystery." But paradoxically, such mystery is not darkness but light. It is the light of divine realities behind the world, throwing material things (bright as these are) into a kind of shadow. This is a shadow which brings out new qualities, new colors.

Just as a hill's lengthened shadow gives a blue-purple tinge to fields that were bright green; and as the impressionist painters, early in our century, showed that shadows themselves are of different hues, so the deeps and shadows of mystery resulting from God's nearness to the world, his working in the world, reveal things in a new way, with new color.

We share, therefore, in the thoughts of the Lord of the gospel, who loved the lilies of the field, and let no sparrow fall uncherished, when, instead of eliminating as much of creation as we can (the way an acrobat does), we rather delight in the immense variety and particularity of things. Then, looking at them with intent and loving gaze, we further find that these varied wonders coalesce into a great unity because of the Father who made and loves them all, and the Son who saw and heard and touched them, and the Spirit who uses them now for his own purposes.

In this book, we are going to look at the world and at God like the leisurely strollers who take time to enjoy the path. This is possible and pleasurable because God is with us as we walk, because God himself is the way we walk, and because walking thus we enjoy him even while we tend towards the ultimate enjoyment of him. Such enjoyment is increased when we have some understanding of four qualities inherent in God's design—qualities of variety, unity, significance, and power. The first of these is variety.

1. *Variety:* "What diversity, Lord, in thy creatures" (Ps. 103)

The treasuring of material things for their own particular qualities is the first kind of delight we have listed. We know how painters and poets down the ages have found joy in such particularity. Nothing in the world is like anything else: fire, for example, is utterly different from water, and in fire itself, light is one thing and warmth is another. Light affects one sense, our sight; warmth affects another—our sense of touch in all its ramifications. We may sometimes enjoy much light (for instance, from an electric lamp) without any appreciable rise in the temperature of the room.

Again, among things of the same species, nothing is completely like anything else: no two leaves, no two sheep, no two curves of waves coming in with the tide. Naturalists even tell us that every dragon fly shows its own characteristics, is different from other dragon flies.

The person who is aware of such individuality, such selfness and inscape, not only loves all leaves, but each leaf, not only all fires, but the shape and glow and color of individual flames. Such sharp individuality cannot be savored in haste. It is good to stop sometimes to feel the unique tingle of one raindrop on the back of a hand, to smell in the evening the always new fragrances of suppers cooking in homes we pass, to differentiate between the soft swish of pines in the wind and the nervous jump and patter of oak trees struck by a sudden breeze.

Because of our tendency to hurry, we sometimes miss this uniqueness in things. Therefore the artist works to arrest us. He thinks that his insight into the special quality of some thing and its design is worthy of our leisured contemplation. Such quiet concentration of our powers is called aesthetic contemplation. It is a delighted and prolonged gaze at something we find beautiful.

Now this same sort of thing is done by the Church in her liturgy. By her use of material things she arrests us; she makes us stop and look at wine and water, oil and bread, wind and fire, and countless other things. Such calling of our attention to the beauty and unity and meaning in things is not the primary end of the liturgy. Its first end is, rather, the channeling of God's power to us, and of our praise to God.

But an aesthetic purpose, an artistic function, is certainly operative in it. Herein, the Church, with Christ, proves that she, moving by the power of the Holy Spirit, is truly an artist with an artist's power of revealing new aspects of things. This is one reason why Dom Herwegen, whom we have quoted earlier, could say that the liturgy has an art principle. "The art principle of the liturgy is transfiguration." It is the glorifying of man and of things that they in turn may glorify God.

Take one instance among hundreds: the lighting of the new fire at Easter. As part of the Easter Vigil ceremonies, a new fire is kindled at the church door. The fire is an ancient symbol for God. He himself chose it as a sign of his presence in the burning bush which Moses saw, in the pillar of fire in the desert, in the fire by which sacrifices in the Old Testament were consumed.

In the New Testament it stands especially for Christ who rose from the rock of his grave as a spark struck from flint. He flashed forth whole and luminous from the bare rock. With these associations lying warm in the back of our minds we are likely to enjoy looking with quiet and intent gaze at particular fires.

When we sit, for example, before a fireplace and watch the blue and yellow flames flicker over the logs, and then see them suddenly roar into redness and swallow up the wood in a flare of sparks, we may think of God as the devouring fire of the Old Testament—of God's greatness and power and transcendence.

Or again, when we have just helped to build a bonfire on a sea cliff, we may look at it and admire its leaping flames, its bright flare, which is, perhaps, visible to ships far out on the ocean. It may be that people out there are cheered or guided by our firelight.

If we have read the Greek dramas we may remember that the rejoicing for Greek victory in the fall of Troy was announced by signal fires which were set ablaze on mountain top after mountain top until the news reached the homeland.

We may next think of the way that God, also, used fire as a signal: he signified his presence and guided his people by a pillar of fire when they were wandering in the desert. This thought, in turn, may call up the psalm that opens the Mass: "Thy light and thy countenance go before me," [12] and so the processes of association set working by the symbol bring us to the fact that we have in the Mass a reminder of the pillar of fire. And this at last suggests to us a present reality—the truth that God is leading us to the promised land of the altar.

All this can be thought more quickly than it can be told. And after the flash of thought we look back at our bonfire with a new delight in its roaring natural beauty and a new love for the firelit faces of our friends gathered around it. With all these associations, and many others, in our conscious or subconscious minds, our appreciation of the natural element of fire is enriched. And even better, our wisdom—our taste and savoring—of the supernatural meaning and power given to fires is increased.

Things, therefore, like the example of fire just given, not only raise our thoughts to God, but their use in the worship of God also leads us to see anew the beauty of things in themselves. This is to say, that when fire or water or words or bread are used in the liturgy, we are not only reminded of God and touched by his power, but we are made newly aware of the earthly thing. It is a two-way process: things and events lead us to God, and God leads us to a new awareness of things—and in this lies adventure.

Such a function of arousing our awareness of the beauty

and value in purely natural things is one of the results of the use of those things in the art structure of the liturgy.

As we go on exploring these notions, little bursts of intensified awareness take place in us. We keep learning to enter more and more fully, through the art qualities of the liturgy, into that part of our heritage which is all the glory of earth and air, fire and water, as well as the joy of heaven. The first of these art-qualities was variety, which we have just been considering. Now let us think about the second, which is unity.

2. *Unity:* "To me, that day, all the morning stars sang together" (Job 38:7)

Not only the earthliness and particularity of natural things brings us delight, but even greater pleasure comes with a perception of the unity which underlies things. To show us a hidden unity, or to shape things into unified wholeness is one of the main purposes of artistic work.

In real life—our everyday world—we are perpetually catching hold of fragments, perpetually being led on from one thing to another. This engenders restlessness, because in life nothing is ever completely finished—new results may spring up at any time. Life is always moving on. Incidents set up chain reactions. We continually see stories begin and seldom find out how they end.

We might compare this feeling of incompleteness to a scene once glimpsed. Perhaps we have seen a girl crying. Does she cry because she must go away, because someone has hurt her, because she dreads the coming of a certain person? The story has no beginning or end. Many questions run through our minds. These questions give rise to the restlessness which belongs to life and its continual flux. Art, on the contrary, either prevents our minds from asking questions by satisfying us immediately (St. Thomas says that beauty is "that which pleases when it is seen"), or else art answers our queries in a way that quiets our restlessness.

If, for example, the weeping girl were a character in a story or a poem, we should know what happened. The incident which caused her sorrow, and its outcome, might be presented to us in unified fashion. Or the scene might be brought before us in such a way that questions would not arise.

The girl's grief, for instance, might be presented as a lovely statue. This is what is done in T. S. Eliot's poem, "La Figlia Che Piange" (The Girl Who Weeps).[18] When we read the poem we are not troubled, but rather we find an artistic pleasure in it. Here are some lines:

> Stand on the highest pavement of the stair—
> Lean on a garden urn—
> Weave, weave the sunlight in your hair—
> Clasp your flowers to you with a pained surprise—
> Fling them to the ground and turn . . .
> But weave, weave the sunlight in your hair.

If we were looking at the statue, we would trace the rhythmic pose of the girl, and the patterns of light and shadow. We would see that the movement is arrested, and so we too would stop and rest.

In reading the poem we feel the rhythm of sound in the rhyme, and the finality of the repeated refrain: "Weave, weave the sunlight in your hair." We are concerned, not with our passing glimpse of her grief, but with the pleasing movement suggested by her pose, and the brightness of the sunlight on her hair. In this same way, even the storm and sorrow of Macbeth or King Lear bring us pleasure, not pain, when they are worked into design and structure—when they become part of a patterned unity.

The reason, therefore, that a good work of art is restful, the reason it furnishes us with the peaceful aesthetic contemplation which has been called "love without desire," lies in its unity. This unity results from the working of a number of factors. Three of them are particularly relevant here. They are, first, framing; second, rhythmic repetition; and third, the device of using a central focus of interest. All of these help to make the object complete and self-sufficient, therefore unified. Let us look at them for a few moments.

Framing comes about, not only when one puts a rectangle or an oval line around a picture by outlining it with wood or contrasting paint, but it can also occur within the very picture itself. For example, an artist sometimes places a central figure or scene between two things: two pillars of an archway, or a tree on one side and a bush or building on the other. These two taller things make a kind of frame—a fence which keeps one's eyes from roving away from the central figure. In this way our attention is focused, and we find ourselves resting in the unity of the painting itself.

Or again, framing in literature is accomplished by arousing a specific need at the beginning of the work and fulfilling it at the end. This is more than a simple resolution of the plot. It may be a statement made early and then repeated with emphasis, or even contradicted at the end.

Take the example of John Donne's poem which begins with an unusual command: "Death be not proud."[14] We wonder if death will obey and humble itself. The poem goes on to pile up arguments, saying that though some have called death "mighty and dreadful," yet it has no reason for pride because kings and wars, poison and sickness can command it to come and it must obey. At last the speaker in the poem says that even the finality, the everlastingness, which death boasts of possessing, is nothing to be proud of because it really does not exist. Death's eternity is not eternal at all.

> One short sleepe past, wee wake eternally,
> And death shall be no more; death, thou shalt die.

Better still is the technique which frames with images instead of statement. Dante's *Divine Comedy*,[15] for instance, begins in a dark forest where he sets out on a painful journey through hell and purgatory. This journey ends when Dante emerges from the last spiral of the purgatorial terraces and finds himself once more in a wood, the bright forest of Eden as it was before the fall. After his adventures in this wood he will be ready to set out on a different journey, a bright journey through the translucent bubbles of the heavens. Here is the opening of the *Inferno* with its description of the dark forest:

> In the middle of the journey of our life
> I came to my senses in a dark forest,
> For I had lost the straight path.
>
> Oh, how hard it is to tell
> what a dense, wild, and tangled wood this was,
> the thought of which renews my fear!

The forest is tangled and gloomy. Here things grow in disorder and confusion. This tangled wood represents the spiritual disorder which is so often characteristic of earthly life.

The tangles of Dante's life are to be untwisted during his penitential journey, and afterwards he will emerge into a "verdant forest," and walk on "fragrant ground" where as he says:

> A sweet unvarying breeze
> touched my face . . . lightly . . .
>
> And made the leaves, quick to tremble,
> bend in the direction
> of the holy mountain's morning shadow . . .
> (*Purg.* 28:7-12)

We see that everything here is bright and ordered. The shadow, for example, is not dense and dark, but it is a "morning shadow"—the word "morning" suggests a certain lightness. The birds, too, "full of joy, greeted the first hours of the day from within the rustling leaves which accompanied their song" (*Purg.* 28:14-18). All is harmony here. Even the leaves do not blow in disorder and independence, but their movement is unified "in the direction of the holy mountain's morning shadow," and their sound blends with and accompanies the singing of the birds.

In this way Dante's journey through hell and purgatory (the penitential part of his pilgrimage) is framed between woods—a dark tangled wood at its beginning and a bright, orderly, harmonious wood at the end.

Such framing occurs in the art of the liturgy, too. We shall see other examples of it later, but for now let us look at just one instance: the framing of the Christian life between two anointings.

The first takes place at baptism, the beginning of the supernatural life. Here one is born of water and the Holy Spirit. This is the beginning of our transfiguration into the likeness of Christ.

The occupation of this life will be a journey taken towards God, and so we are strengthened at the outset, made ready for the road, by this first anointing. (During the journey we are anointed again at confirmation, and perhaps a third time in holy orders—these mark special stages on the journey, and special transformations of the wayfarer.)

Then at the end of the series of anointings, at the end of the journey, we receive the last anointing. Normally this sacrament of extreme unction should complete the transfiguration begun at baptism. By its power we should be at last truly transfigured Christians, wholly assimilated to the transfigured Christ.

If the Christian has the proper receptivity, this anointing prepares the soul for entrance into heaven. It should be an immediate preparation for beatitude, an "anointing unto glory," as St. Thomas says (Cont. Gent. iv, 73). After this, the Christian, like Dante, is ready to begin the last bright journey into the presence of God. In this way, the Christian life is framed between two very important anointings.

There are other kinds of framing also in the liturgy. Such control which results in unity can be further seen in the stability and inclusiveness of the circular pattern which will be discussed in the next chapter. In a certain way, the circle itself functions as a kind of frame.

The second unifying principle is that of rhythm. This is patterned repetition or measured movement. We know how natural and pleasing rhythm is to man. For one thing, we talk and walk and breathe in a rhythmic pattern which differs for each of us. For another, we instinctively impose patterns of rhythm on all kinds of things: on movement in the dance, on sound when we shape words or musical tones into the cadenced rise and fall of poetry and song or into the more intricate designs of musical structure.

In both life and the arts rhythm is based on the expectancy of repetition. A desire is roused in us for the recurrence of something—perhaps a color or a sound. Then when we meet it again, maybe in a slightly different form, but still recognizable, we are pleased. An example of this repetition with variation is that of rhyme in poetry.

Or again we might think of the repetitions in nature. All our lives we have seen the sun rise, and we base our patterns of behavior on the fact that we expect it to rise on each tomorrow. We have watched the moon grow slim and fill out again, and trees lose their leaves and grow them again. We feel comfortable when our lives, too, fall into a regular and ordered pattern. True, we enjoy doing different and unusual things on holidays, but we return home and find there is something pleasant about doing things at regular times and knowing just what to expect.

With rhythm, furthermore, we form all kinds of visual

patterns. In a cathedral like Chartres, for example, the varied repetition of the vertical lines creates an upward soaring rhythm which helps one to enter into an attitude of adoration. Such patterning emphasizes the transcendence, the otherness of God. On the other hand, the rhythm of rounded domes, like that we see in the Roman style of churches, brings to mind God's immanence, his bending down from heaven to take loving care of us.

Again, we see a different use of rhythm in such a picture as Grant Woods' "The Midnight Ride of Paul Revere." Here, even if the horseman were covered up, one could still feel a galloping rhythm. The speed and movement are captured in the road that curves quickly up and down over the hills, and in the repetition of this larger curve in the shorter curves of the hills and the circular lines of the trees.

In another fashion still, the pictures which illustrate this book are patterned in a serene and peaceful rhythm. Partly this is the result of the long steady lines. The centurion, for example, was first drawn with a number of quick nervous lines in his armor. This made the picture seem too full of flighty movement to suit a man of such strong and serene faith. When the artist changed the rhythm of the lines, the whole mood became different.

The harmony and balance of these illustrations (both of which qualities are aspects of rhythm) are observable in the placement of all their lines and masses. Such permeating of a whole picture by a particular rhythm helps the work of art to be true to its subject, and also acts as a unifying agent.

The Church, too, uses rhythm. We shall spend some time later tracing the pattern she follows when she invites us to pray in harmony with the natural rhythms of the rise and fall of light, and the recurring seasons of the year. This patterned repetition is the principle, moreover, on which themes—themes in poetry, music, painting—operate. We shall see such a theme in action when, in chapter three, we treat the central purpose of the liturgy which is Christian transfiguration.

A third unifying principle is that of centralizing the whole design around a focal point, a center of interest to which everything is drawn and from which an influence goes out to all the rest of the work. In a picture, this may be a bright spot of color, or a particular curve; in a piece of music, a melodic phrase.

Just such a center is found in the liturgy. In it, Christ is both a centripetal, magnetizing force, and a centrifugal, radiating power, transfiguring all by the influence which emanates from him, and drawing all things to himself. This centrality of Christ will be the subject of chapter five.

Such discoveries of unified design in art furnish a unique pleasure. This pleasure also comes to us sometimes in the happenings of our lives. Think of the serene joy which floods us when we find things fitting together in new relationships, when we discover a perfectly right and unifying principle for some set of disparate ideas, objects, or actions.

Perhaps we ourselves have been obsessed by some problem. We have been persistently and vaguely irritated because we could not see how the details of a poem, a picture, a geometry theorem, or the elements in some problem of human relationships could fit together. We have pursued one detail, then another, but they have never formed a whole for us.

Then finally we discover that our very worrying at the puzzle, our impatient probing at the object embedded in our mind, is all the while causing the object to become englobed within us, like a pearl formed by our irritation. And at last, on one day of revelation, everything comes clear: one obscure poem makes sense; the painting which seemed to be dismembered all over the canvas emerges as a new unity; the problem in human relationships is solved, and we walk into a new room full of peace.

Now we find ourselves possessed of a warm and perfect

sphere of understanding. Our knowledge is rounded out into a satisfying whole. And we say to ourselves that we have in truth found a pearl of great price.

Think of this realization of unity in another way. We know that there are a million (and more) scattered stars in the heavens, and each possesses its own beauty. But when we become aware of them as great interwheeling worlds circling about each other, drawn into certain orbits because of each other, then we see them glorified into even greater harmony of interrelating rhythm and pattern. Then we admire the way in which they obey

> ... those laws, stupendous and balancing,
> Which made the hurl of smiting, infamous fires
> Wheel in perfection, perpetually,
> In great unaltering constellations . . .[16]

Moreover, the wider the complexity and variety of things which are unified, the richer is the whole which they form. The *Divine Comedy* of Dante, for example, is a poem which combines the richest complexity of detail with a large and sure clarity of structure and design. It is this achievement of shaping many disparate experiences into one admirable whole, that makes the poem so deeply satisfying to generation after generation of readers. Dante is a master in perfect control of the unifying principles of framing, rhythm, and central focus.

Not only does Dante create a poem which is magnificently unified, but he is enchanted by the unity which he sees in God's even greater design, and he describes this insight in wonderful images.

For example, before he comes to his final vision of unity, Dante has made a journey through the world of the dead. He has gone down, spiral by spiral, into the varied horrors of hell, being assaulted in every one of his senses by his experiences there. He has climbed the seven terraces of the purgatorial mountain, meeting every kind of person, hearing strange songs, and enjoying the fragrance of new varieties of flowers. Finally, he has circled through the infinite variety of the motion, music, and light in the concentric and transparent bubbles of the heavens.

He has undergone a multiplicity of experiences. And yet he does succeed in unifying them, for at the end of the journey he comes to the vision of the highest heavens. There he sees all the scattered leaves of the whole universe bound together in a book of God's making. He describes the vision by saying that he fixed his eyes on the Eternal Light, and then he tells us:

> In its depths I saw contained, bound with love
> in one volume, what is scattered
> on leaves throughout the world.
> *(Paradiso,* 33:85-87)

It is as if God, in creation, had been writing a book, putting into it all the variety of beings he had made, and finally, at the consummation, binding all the pages into one majestic volume.

Dante, it is true, is a great poet. He was able to make a unity out of the tremendous variety of things in his poem, and he was also able to find and grasp the unity in God's work of art, which is creation. We, on the other hand, are quite ordinary people. Nevertheless, some power of unifying our awareness of a rich and varied universe can be ours also. A comparable, if lesser, insight is possible for each of us. And the three principles of framing, rhythm, and focus of interest can help us to find that sense of rest in unity which is the gift of art to man.

Painting, music, sculpture, even the dance give us such pleasure by furnishing an opportunity for us to rest in contemplation of their whole and self-enclosed unity. But this kind of rest is also activity. It is a heightened awareness—a peak of life which is intense but serene.

We can have such insight when we contemplate the ordering, the pattern and unity, in the Church's system of worship. Here all materials and all patterns of movement are designed into a system of concentric circles. This is a kind of over-all framing, a unified and controlled design. All these things, moreover, are informed by a single purpose and are thus possessed of a central focus—Christ and his activity of transfiguration. And finally they are made palpable by the use of reiterated symbols and meaningful by repetition of themes. Both of these recur with satisfying rhythm.

By grasping these elements of structure and design, and then tracing the unifying theme and interwoven symbols in the liturgy, we can begin to see creation as united in one great praiseful whole. Then no longer will Mass and sacraments and fasts and feasts be isolated from each other, nor their true meaning be cut off from work and meals and all our daily living.

Things will rather emerge as closely related, informed by a central purpose, and patterned into design. Within this design we shall see that each part of our worship of God is interrelated with all the others, and each aspect of sacrament and sacrifice (the two main elements of the liturgy) glorifies and enriches even the small details of our daily living.

Some of these relationships will be pointed out in the pages that follow. Others will come into focus as we live our lives in growing awareness of what Christopher Fry, in *The Boy with a Cart*, calls "divinity working above the wind, working under our feet." Then, as he puts it in the same play, "coming out from doorways on April evenings . . . watching the lark dissolve in the sun" we shall more and more feel "heaven ride with spring into the meadows." [17]

3. *Significance:* "a world having deeps and shadows of mystery."

Besides the adventure of discovering the unity and variety of things in the world, we are also made glad by finding significance in them. "Creation is full of expectancy" (Rom. 8:19), waiting for God to manifest himself in it. This is one kind of significance man has long felt. And this expectancy is being fulfilled from moment to moment.

Man has a strong tendency to feel that unseen powers move in things, that the universe carries secret messages meant for individual human beings. For one thing, it gives us a sense of security to feel that the stars are mindful of us. Perhaps this longing is a desire to feel God's providence watching over us. Perhaps by calling on the mountains to shield us we are not only remembering the way that mountain valleys are sheltered from cold winds, but we are also striving to heal our smallness by a sense that these great creatures, the mountains, bend themselves to serve us.

Then again, since it is true, as the proverb says, that "God is the country of the soul," it is understandable that all our lives we should be seeking for signs which will bring us here and now into this country which is our true home. We seek meanings in things because we are restless, because consciously or unconsciously we are always searching for God.

As St. Augustine said, "Thou hast made us for thyself, O God, and our hearts are restless until they rest in thee." If God really is the country of the soul, the only one in whom we can find healing for our restlessness, then it is no wonder that we seek for glimpses of another world, for answers to our questions about earth's relations to infinity.

Then, too, the earth is so filled with wonders that we feel a sense of waste when we imagine that this lovely surface is everything. We want it to be beautiful, but we also desire that it should have a deeper, a transmaterial value. And so it has.

This search for significance is natural to man. We see the girl pulling sunflower petals and half-playfully, half-prayerfully wondering: "He loves me; he loves me not." We find the ancient pagans looking for portents, and for indications of the will of the gods in the flight of birds. And from earliest times the study of the stars has tempted man to discover a hidden meaning and a hidden power in their patterned movement.

The psalmist says: "See how the skies proclaim God's glory, how the vault of heaven betrays his craftsmanship" (Ps. 18); and again, "The light is a garment thou dost wrap about thee, the heavens a curtain thy hand unfolds" (Ps. 103). The constant theme, in fact, of the psalms and of many Old Testament prophecies is this glory of God signified by and shining out from the material world.

In the world of the liturgy, significances not only allude to deeper meaning and reveal it; they not only point to "divinity working above the wind, working under our feet" (to repeat Fry's words), but here the signs are more than just meanings. They are also facts. The sacraments function to transform man and the world on the supernatural level. They do this in a way related to the sign used. Therefore the sign itself is important.

It is important because it means something: water means cleansing and fertility for crops; bread means nourishment, and shared bread means fellowship. And the sign is even more important because it functions as God's instrument in producing the effect signified—such effects as spiritual cleansing and new life, nourishment and communal oneness.

This is what is meant by the familiar definition: sacraments are signs which effect what they signify. Since this is so, since the meanings of the symbolic words, acts, materials, are not only brought to mind but are effected, caused, actually happen in those concerned—then the signification must be important.

The material and design of the sacrament even, in a certain way, shape the grace received. It therefore makes a difference what sign—what material and what pattern of words and action—is used. Think of it this way: a tree is to be cut down. It may be done with an axe or a saw. In either case, the effect will be accomplished. The tree will be felled. But the trunk will be marked differently according to the different instrument used. In an analogous fashion, we may say that the actions and materials used in effecting sacramental grace leave their mark on the recipient.

Baptism, for example, might have been given under other signs. It might have been administered (had Christ so planned it) by having a person stand in a bright light, thus pouring light on him instead of water. Or the grace of the sacrament could have become effective purely by words, or by silent prayer. But it is given by water. And the significance of water, as shall be seen later, has much to do with the kind of grace received.

Again, take the sign of bread for an example. Bread means food; food serves to nourish, to invigorate, to delight. If a sacrament comes clothed in the sign of bread, we can expect that its grace will nourish, vivify, and delight our souls.

The sign of bread, furthermore, also suggests a meal. And meals are not normally taken alone. Generally they are communal affairs—social gatherings as well as occasions for renewing the body's strength. This means that some notion of sharing with others, of being united with others, must be signified by the Bread of the Eucharist. And so it is. St. Paul puts it clearly: "The one bread makes us one body, though we are many in number" (I Cor. 10:17).

The definition of a sacrament, moreover, as a sign which effects what it signifies, is also true in a lesser degree and on a different level in the other elements of the liturgy. For example, the consecration of the day by the circling hours of the official praise of God, and the hallowing of the year by the changing liturgical seasons—all these also cause certain changes, certain transformations, in man and in nature.

In these cyclical patterns, the whole world of earth, air, fire, and water is gathered up and glorified by actual liturgical use, and also by the words of the psalms, which call upon every kind of creature to praise God. The patterns of the rise and fall of light, of the birth and burgeoning and diminishing of the year, unify and become a sign of hallowing for all the things of time and space. Here, too, though in a different way from the sacraments themselves, those things which are signified are also caused—and therefore the sign itself becomes important.

The whole sacramental and sacrificial world of the liturgy is, then, full of significance. Different aspects of this significance will be treated in later chapters, especially in chapter four on symbolism, and in the last chapters which study the actual words and actions of the sacraments, office, and seasons.

This effectiveness of signs—of words, acts, materials—in the liturgy is in reality the power of Christ working in and through them: "In Christ the whole plentitude of Deity is embodied, and dwells in him, and it is in him that you find your completion; he is the fountain head from which all dominion and power proceed" (Col. 2:9-11). With some aspects of this power we shall next be concerned. This is the fourth and last of the qualities which we listed at the beginning of this chapter.

4. *Power:* "He whose power is at work in us is powerful enough, and more than powerful enough, to carry out his purpose beyond all our hopes and dreams" (Eph. 3:20-21).

Not only do words and actions and material things point up meanings in the supernatural world—not only do they signify. They also cause events and transformations to happen. They, by God's power working through them and in them, effect what they signify.

Not only do they call things to our minds and memories, but when they are used in the liturgy they re-present, they make present in our time and space, the power of Christ, through his body which is the Church. Christ, in other words, acts here and now in this, his mystical body, by using some sensible sign. In using this sign he affects not only our senses, but our spirits too.

Christ our Lord, for example, acted with power during his life on earth. He healed illness, quieted storms, changed water into wine. He did these things by means of that body which he had taken from our humanity—a body belonging to our time and space. He performed these actions of his historical life by using the body which he had received from his mother.

He used his feet to go on errands of mercy ("Our friend Lazarus is at rest now; I am going there to awake him" John 11:11-12), and to carry truth to men ("That day, leaving the house, Jesus had sat down by the sea shore, and great multitudes gathered about him . . . and he spoke to them" Matt. 13:1-3). He touched sinners and sufferers with his hands of flesh ("And he laid his hands upon each one of them" Luke 4:40). He looked, through his bodily eyes, with compassion or with sternness at those he would save ("The Lord turned and looked at Peter" Luke 22:61).

But now he has, as it were, stepped outside time and space. "Now he has gone up, high above the heavens," as St. Paul says (Eph. 4:10-11), but Paul adds immediately that he has done this in order to "fill creation with his presence." He is at the right hand of the Father, but we are still on the earth. We human beings are incurably of earth, immersed in materiality—and rightly so, for thus God made us: body and soul.

Therefore, in order that the glorified Christ and earthbound human beings may, as it were, "make contact," Christ now in effecting the works of his power, uses a body which is, like us, immersed in time and space. This body through which he works to transform men is his mystical body, the Church—the "whole Christ," in St. Augustine's famous phrase.

By means of this body, through which Christ truly acts, the signs (words, acts, materials) which the Church uses are made powerful to effect what they signify.

The sacrificial and sacramental banquet of the Mass, for example, actually nourishes the individual soul, and also unites and strengthens the whole body of Christ because it is a meal taken in togetherness.

On a different level, such other aspects of the liturgy as the consecration of the day and year also, as we have said, effect what they signify, each in its own way and to its own degree. The soul, for example, wakes at dawn, not only to a new day on earth, but to a renewal of the life of grace. The Christian goes out, because of the power of the Church's prayer, with new energy to praise and work for God. And he comes home at evening "carrying sheaves" the harvest of holiness reaped during the day.

Again, the Christian rises anew with each resurrection festival of Eastertide, matures and produces fruit by means of Pentecostal grace, presents his good deeds as a harvest to God, and begins with Advent (in the winter) to look forward to a new coming, a new revelation of Christ. When this revelation comes with the Nativity, he commemorates not only the newly born Savior, but he also rejoices in anticipation of Christ's final triumphal coming at the end of time.

By the power of Christ, who acts in the liturgy, these acts (made effective once for all during his life on earth) now dip down into our time and space, as it were, so that we can touch them. Not only do they recall happenings to our minds and memories, but they re-present, re-activate for our special benefit, the very events themselves. They cause Christ to relive his life in us in such true fashion that we can say with St. Paul: "I live, now not I, but Christ lives in me."

Because of this power which emanates from Christ and draws all things to him, we see him as the center of the liturgical design. Around him wheel the four great circles of Mass, sacraments, office, and year. Some of the meanings which men have seen in circles, will therefore be our concern as we begin the next chapter.

CHAPTER TWO

Of Circles and the Design of the Liturgy

> I saw eternity the other night
> Like a great ring of pure and
> endless light.
>
> HENRY VAUGHAN [18]

> Within the deep and clear subsistence
> of the great light [the Trinity] three
> circles of three colors
> and of one dimension appeared to me.
>
> *Paradiso*, 33:15-17

DEEP IN MAN'S NATURE is the instinct to see in the circle a symbol for things which are always changing, always in flux, yet always stable and secure. This is the reason for our suggesting that one key to the unifying of all creation in the Church's system of worship is a design based on circles. The circle, as seen in the pattern of the liturgy, signifies and unifies. Within its movement, each kind of sacrificial and sacramental reality acts according to its own nature to transfigure man through the power of God.

1. *The circle as a natural image*

The circle is, first of all, a basic natural figure. Think of the fascination people experience in watching a stone dropped in still water. There is quietude in the circles which move out and out from the center. And at the same time there is delight in the rhythmical lapping of each circle as it washes outward and then curves down in return—as it suggests completeness in itself, and at the same time sets in motion another larger circle.

Think, too, of whirlpools. Whether they are mere dimples on the surface of a pool, or whether they are engulfing swirls of water, people will stand and stare. These curves are always going someplace, and yet they are always there.

Again, how fitting it was that God should use the half-circle of the rainbow as his symbol of peace—as a reminder to himself to protect his people from his own wrath. He says, "I will set my bow in the clouds, in those clouds my bow shall appear, to remind me of my promise to you, and to all the life that quickens mortal things; never shall the waters rise in flood again, and destroy all living creatures. There, in the clouds, my bow shall stand, and as I look upon it, I will remember this eternal covenant" (Gen. 10:13-16).

Is it a wonder, then, that from early times men have drawn magic circles for protection around themselves and their flocks. Christopher Fry describes such a scene in *The Boy with a Cart*:

> . . . . I took
> My crook, and round the sheep I drew a circle
> Saying "God guard them here, if God will guard them";
> Drew it, though as a fence I knew it was less
> Good than a bubble? [19]

The idea of the circle as protection could well have been suggested by the arc of the rainbow which embraces man and his works and seems to keep all safe.

The rainbow presages peace as well as protection. Perhaps its prism trembles over the rocky chaos of a mountain. At its touch all the crags dissolve into serenity. Every jutting corner and harsh surface is softened by its light. Its magic seems to be quieting the wrath and struggle suggested by the violently upthrust rocks. With its appearance, the great beast of a mountain lies down like a lamb.

Then sometimes on the desert, or over green fields, one may watch another peaceful rainbow picture. Perhaps a wide winged bird comes from nowhere and sails slowly against the sky, patterning his tilted circles against the vertical arc of the rainbow. The rainbow remains still, the bird moves; the rainbow is upright, the bird's circles are tipped now one way and now another.

The bird, like Hopkins' "Windhover," in his "riding of the rolling level underneath him steady air," draws our eyes, and yet we are always conscious of the quietly glimmering rainbow in the background. In the scene we find a fullness of satisfaction, a realization of activity and quietude. And this special pleasure comes from the movement outward and the return which is characteristic of circles, as well as from the play of light and color in the scene.

There are other kinds of circles too. What awe we feel sometimes, looking up under the stars at night and thinking of the centripetal force which holds all these huge worlds in their patterned orbits. Then we think, tomorrow night and forever, it will be like this. Yet it will be forever changing too, as the satellites change their courses around their suns.

The psalmist says, "See how the skies proclaim God's glory, how the vault of heaven betrays his craftsmanship" (Ps. 18:2). And we, watching the vault of heaven, are quieted even while we realize our own smallness. And at the same time we feel honored to be witness of so much majesty.

In another place (Baruch 3:33-36), we find that God called the muster-roll of the stars, and they answered his call. "It is on his errand that the light goes forth, his summons that it obeys with awe; joyfully the stars shine out, keeping the watches he has appointed, answer when he calls their muster-roll, and offer their glad radiance to him who fashioned them." Their joyful answer to God's call is phrased in the beautiful obedience of their everlasting circles. Perhaps this is what the ancients meant when they talked of the music of the spheres: it was the song of joyful surrender sung by the great wheeling worlds.

The movement of time, too, is patterned in circles. We, along with all the generations of our ancestors, see the sun come up at dawn and move in a circle which encloses the world. And when it has gone below the flat counter-curve of the horizon at night, we follow it in our minds, down out of sight, and we feel that the whole round world is encircled and bound together by its shining path.

This same rhythm of rise and return occurs in the cycle of the year's seasons. Spring comes: things rise to renewed life; they ripen and mature with summer, are ready for harvest in fall, and sink to quietude in the winter. Then the cycle begins again.

Someone has said, in this regard, that the reason modern man finds a new restlessness in himself is that he is not able to identify himself with the cycles of nature, but lives instead on a never-ending line. Ancient man entered into the spirit of each varying season by necessity, since he lived so close to the soil, and could not control the weather's manifestations.

Medieval man likewise lived in a natural cycle of seasons, but he also lived very vividly the seasons of supernatural life —the variety of fasts and feasts in the liturgical year. But modern man, in the concrete canyons of our cities, is far from the cycles of earth's variation and stability. And he often feels lost and hopeless.

Recurrence does give rise to hope. We know how new hope springs continually in us because of the constant return and renewal of the days and seasons. How often, for example, after a day has gone badly, do we not console ourselves with the thought that tomorrow will be better. On the other hand, it is true, as the scholars tell us, that ancient man was sometimes enslaved by the monotony of the cycle of nature's recurrences and lost his hope. This can happen if one remains always on the purely natural level.

In the supernatural cycle, however, there is not this same danger of monotony. For in living it, we do not everlastingly follow the same path, but we view and enter into the recurring mysteries each time from another vantage point, another level.

Since our sharing in them transfigures us, changes us in a very real way, we come to them each time almost as different persons. Our progress is rather like spiralling around a mountain. We see the same things, but each time from a higher place, and with new eyes, and so we see them differently and they affect us differently. In the circle of man's life which begins at birth, rounds out into maturity, and gradually diminishes with old age, there are, therefore, these many smaller circles of time which affect him on both natural and supernatural levels.

2. *The circle as symbol: its meaning*

In all these natural circles, two paradoxically different concepts present themselves. These are the notions of stillness and movement. When, for example, we see a wheel we think immediately of progressing motion, of movement toward a goal. Yet at the same time we know that at the center of the wheel is a stationary point which gives it stability. T. S. Eliot presents this concept by means of an image which unites the world of nature and the world of faith. He says this center is "the still point of the turning world. . . . Except for the point, the still point, / There would be no dance, and there is only the dance. . . . [Here one is] surrounded / by a grace of sense, a white light, still and moving." [20]

We also know that the circumference or rim of the wheel,

though it travels on indefinitely, will not stretch out and disappear in the distance, but it will return upon itself. This too makes for stability and security. From this meaning, perhaps, we derive the symbolism of the ring as unfailing constancy through all days and all change.

Just so, the sacramental universe is perpetually renewed. It responds in infinitely varied ways to each man's needs, and yet it is stable. It is the one redemption won by Christ, never changing, yet ever new in each man's time and space.

Another kind of satisfying security comes from the symbolic meaning of completion or wholeness. A circle has no sharp angles or corners, therefore no inequalities. It has no breaks in its roundness, and is utterly finished, complete in itself, equal in every part, filled up with sufficiency.

"With this ring I thee wed," says the bridegroom. And the ring stands for the wholeness of his love—its permanence and fidelity. It symbolizes the completion which comes to man and woman in marriage because each is complementary to the other, each fulfills the other. It means also the continuing progress combined with unchanging stability of the love they pledge to each other.

Poets in particular have made use of the paradox of the circle's symbolism. Henry Vaughan, in the seventeenth century, tries with it to capture the ineffable meaning of eternity which is ever the same, ever fully possessed, yet ever new.

He says, "I saw eternity the other night / Like a great ring of pure and endless light . . . / And round beneath it, Time, in hours, days, years / Driv'n by the spheres." At the end of the poem he explains his symbol by telling us that this circle of eternity is the nuptial ring which God the Bridegroom provides for the soul of man: "This Ring the Bridegroom did for none provide / But for his bride." [21]

John Donne, also, writing about the same time, uses the circle and the still point at its center to picture two earthly lovers. He says they are like the two parts of a draughtsman's

OF CIRCLES AND THE DESIGN OF THE LITURGY

compass. The beloved remains still—a steadfast point in the center of the circle made by the lover. And when he must go away, all his movements are governed by her steadfastness.

> Our two soules . . . .
> If they be two, they are two so
>   As stiffe twin compasses are two,
> Thy soule, the fixt foot, makes no show
>   To move, but doth, if the other doe.
>
> And though it in the center sit,
>   Yet when the other far doth rome,
> It leans, and hearkens after it. . . .
>
> Such wilt thou be to mee, who must
>   Like th' other foot, obliquely runne;
> Thy firmnes makes my circle just,
>   And makes me end, where I begunne.[22]

Dante also heaps up images in his *Paradiso*, seeking in this way to describe the peace and yet the complete actuality and activity of the heavens and of God. One of his favorite images is the circle. A particularly beautiful instance occurs in canto thirty.

The poet has just been blinded by the vivid light of heaven, and Beatrice, his guide, tells him that "the love which quiets this heaven always welcomes with such a greeting." Heaven, in other words, always strikes the new arrival with a temporary blindness. But this is done for the purpose of strengthening his sight. "In order," as she says, "to make the candle fit for its flame."

Then Dante finds himself "surmounting his own power." He says, "New vision was kindled in me. . . . and I saw radiance like a river flowing between two banks." Beautiful as is the moving river of light, however, it is but "a shadowy preface of the reality." And even while he watches, the river turns, and begins to form a circle. It "changes its length . . .

into something round." And "the flowers and sparks change ... into greater festival."

As the river of light "extends in the form of a circle," he sees it gradually shaping itself into a great white rose, of which God is the burning center in the heart of light, and all the blessed form the petals which surround him.

This is one of the most beautiful passages in literature. In it we see in a new way the movement and stability, the enclosure and peace, yet the living dynamism of the circle's meaning.

3. *The circle in the world of worship*

Now this very old and majestic symbol of a center surrounded by concentric circles is the design which has been chosen here to illustrate the structural unity of the world of worship.

The circle is especially appropriate to the world of sacramental and sacrificial reality because here we have the unchanging Christ acting, and these everlasting yet ever new actions of his are applied to man in the flux of human life. Even the great God—he whom Dante describes as "the Love which moves the sun and other stars" in their unwearying circles—is symbolized by the wholeness, stability, and dynamism of the circle.

In such symbolism is mystery enough to send one's mind hovering in a circling and contemplative gaze. Such thought is rather like a bird's hover. And engaged in such a meditative hover, "between birth and death we may touch understanding / As a moth brushes a window with its wing." So Christopher Fry describes such glimpses into mystery.[23]

Let us think of the image of a bird's hovering from a different point of view than that we took earlier. It may be that one day you have seen a hawk circling against the sky. It moves its wings now and then, but most of the time it sails serenely, watching and waiting with unflickering patience. It is getting ready to swoop down on some small animal. All its slow repetition will come at last to this swift pounce.

In a movement like the bird's, we too can draw out a thought in unhurried peace, in a kind of circling, alternating as the bird does between flight and hovering. All the time we are keeping a quiet gaze fixed on the object of our interest or admiration. We are waiting until the perfect moment of illumination comes. Then we can grasp, in a swift intuitive pounce, the deep reality of the thing we have been contemplating and make it our own.

This kind of thought is particularly fitted for the enjoyment of beauty—natural beauty made by God, artistic beauty shaped by man's intelligent mind and manual skill, or the mysterious beauty of the Creator himself. By such thought we delight and unify and quiet our minds.

By this kind of thought we delight in trees and wide treeless spaces, in looming mountains or incoming tide. And it is also by this kind of thought that we lose ourselves and our small concerns in admiring contemplation of works of art: noticing how color contrasts with color, curve balances curve, small pattern emerges from and enriches the large whole.

Best of all, it is by such circular thinking that we can contemplate the deep "mine of God's wisdom, of his knowledge" and admire his "undiscoverable ways" (Rom. 11:33). By it, we can penetrate into the "mystery kept hidden from the beginning of time in the all creating mind of God" (Eph. 3:9).

In such thought, which is the kind we shall be doing through most of the book, the eyes and mind move, not in smooth forward fashion, as in the reading of clear prose, but in a repetitive pattern marked by spurts and lingerings. When we do this we stop now and then to re-view one aspect, to catch echoes in meaning and color from different sections of the landscape or poem or symphony. We trace what someone has named "little calls here and there in the structure."

This circular thinking is the kind that the Church encourages us to use in our prayerful reading of scripture, and especially in the whole system of her worship of God. And one of the techniques she constantly employs to lead us to such a-logical, contemplative, circular thought, is that of presenting her meaning to us through recurrent images and symbols.

She will, for example, mention bread (as in the Lord's Prayer at Mass), then move on and suggest home and the sharing of bread in the "Domine non sum dignus" ("I am not worthy that Thou shouldst enter under my roof"—that you should partake of my hospitality); then she will pray that we may have increase of life from the nourishment of the heavenly bread.

Bread and home and life are all connected with each other, but we proceed to find their interrelationships by an a-logical progress from symbol to symbol (a kind of hovering) rather than by syllogistic thinking. This is the kind of suggestion by association which many modern poets use.

Such thought is not the only kind our minds can know, but it is one kind. And it is valuable to us because it can enrich our powers of praying, add a new dimension to our knowing, and help us to organize and unify our worship of God into a satisfying wholeness.

On a system of circles, therefore, we shall base our thinking about the design of the liturgy. A circle suggests, as has been said, movement and quietude, continual progression along with perfect completion. The point at its center is unchanging, yet the whole moving circle depends upon it.

In our design Christ is the center, the point. This idea of God as a point is very old. Julian of Norwich, for example, who lived in the middle ages, says, "I saw God in a Point ... by which sight I saw that he is in all things." Christ is the point, the center, because in him humanity and divinity meet. More than this, he is the unchanging being of God made visible to us in the changing form of our humanity.

We know that "What Jesus Christ was yesterday, and is today, he remains for ever" (Heb. 13:8). And we know too that his mercy adapts itself to each man, and to every circumstance. He brings "peace [for those] far off, peace for those who [are] near" (Eph. 2:17). On him the whole sacramental and sacrificial system of worship depends. He is the one who acts in the perpetual movement of the circles, and it is he who gives them their completion and stability.

The concentric circles which surround Christ the center are, first and nearest to him, the unchanging yet perpetually renewed sacrifice of the Mass. Here is found Christ's own worship of the Father, and here is "brought within our reach" (as the liturgy says) the Savior himself for our joy and peace.

The second circle is that of man's life as its beginning, maturing, and completion is consecrated through the sacramental system. Third comes the circle of the day, which is given variety and significance by the Hours of the divine office, based on the symbolism of the day's circling light.

Finally, the fourth circle is that of the liturgical year with its progressing seasons, which bring the different aspects of Christ's life to us in an ever repeated yet ever new motion. Here we shall find that the year with its three seasons moves in an ascending system of climaxes from darkness to light at Christmastide, from death to life at Easter, and from light and life to a flaming out of love at Pentecost.

In each of these circles, one theme operates to unify all the rich variety, to give significance to the whole, and to transform the world by God's power. This is the theme of transfiguration. It keynotes all of Christianity, and has, as we shall see in the next chapter, special functions in regard to God, man, and the rest of the created world.

CHAPTER THREE

Of Transfiguration: the Theme of the Liturgy

> ... a transformation into a radiant likeness of the divinity is effected by the fire of the Holy Spirit into which we are plunged.
> SCHEEBEN [24]
>
> The idea of Christian transfiguration is the art-principle of the liturgy.
> HERWEGEN [25]

JUST AS the one design of the circle both informs the worship of God with a meaning of perpetuity and recurrence, and at the same time symbolizes the unity and wholeness of God's design for our saving, so the theme of transfiguration is related in many ways to our worship, and permeates the whole of the liturgy.

This theme reveals in a new light the variety and particularity of things, and shows new meaning underlying them. It helps to weld all this variousness into unity, and expresses the effect of God's power which works in and through the words, acts, and materials of the liturgy.

Such transfiguration is first of all the gradual transformation of Christians into the likeness of Christ. It is also, in another way, a transforming of nature—an investing of all things with new glory and a new value. It is brought about by God, who uses natural instruments for his purposes, and it is slower or swifter, more or less complete, according to man's cooperation.

We have called the idea of transfiguration a theme—the theme of the liturgy. Let us see, first of all, how themes can be expected to function. After that we will study the particular theme of transfiguration itself.

1. *Themes: the way they function*

Themes in the plastic arts, in music, and in literature, function according to a principle of more or less rhythmical recurrence; that is, through the satisfying of expectancy by repetition with variation. Music, for example, proposes to the listener a thread of melody, a certain harmony, a rhythmic structure. With this as a foundation, the mood of the music may vary. In one case, it may express sadness by being phrased in a minor key; and then, with the same basic melody, harmony, and rhythm, by a change of instruments or key, it may suggest liveliness or a solemn ceremonial march.

Take Brahms' "Variations on a Theme by Haydn," for example. In this piece there are eight variations on one single theme, and then a ringing close where the melody and harmony of the fundamental theme emerge in clear statement, celebrated by a booming of bells.

The theme itself suggests an ancient song for pilgrims, and is both grave and charming. In each variation, the first five bars of this melody can be heard, but each time, the orchestra moves on to the variations, leaving the theme incomplete. This gives a cumulative suspense to the whole. Every time our expectancy is aroused, it is partially (but never completely) satisfied, until we come to the end.

So it is with man's transfiguration into the likeness of

Christ. In each sacrament, at each Mass, during each festal season, the theme—the actuality, rather—of transfiguration is presented, and each time it is carried a little further, but it is not complete until the soul is finally ready for the beatific vision.

By repetition, themes sometimes serve as devices for framing, and so they add to the unity of some segment of reality. The Brahms piece, for example, is framed. The first variation on the theme is softly animated, and it looks forward to the end because it is filled with bell-like echoes. At the close of the piece, these echoes are actualized when the bells ring out and the theme is triumphantly played through to the end.

In a similar way man's life is framed. He receives a beginning of transfiguration at baptism. At this time he first shares in the supernatural life. But it is only at the end of his life, when the last anointing has made him ready for the beatific vision, that the final statement of the theme comes. Only then does his life reach its final triumphant unity.

Somewhat in this fashion, themes may operate in poems. Let us take Dylan Thomas' "Fern Hill" [26] as an example of theme and variations. In this poem the theme is one of the transience of joy. The poem says that children are happy, but when they grow up they lose childhood's innocence and its joy. The first lines are joyous: "O as I was young and easy under the apple boughs / About the lilting house / And happy as the farm was home." Here the poet states openly the first half of the theme: I was happy.

Then the other half, that of the loss of joy, is presented by implication: "Time let me / Hail and climb." That is, Time, which has the child in its power, is merciful for the moment. It "lets" him play and be happy. This is merely temporary toleration, however, and before the poem is ended Time will snatch away the joy.

After the first lines, come differences in the mode of presentation. Along with the direct statement of joy and its transience, the theme is presented concretely by means of two symbols: the farm in daylight stands for joy, and the carrying away of the farm by darkness symbolizes the loss of joy. The first time the farm vanishes, the loss is temporary. It returns, and the child at dawn sees "the farm come back, the cock on his shoulder."

But at the end of the poem the loss of the farm and of joy is permanent, for now the "children green and golden /Follow [Time] out of grace." At last the child realizes his loss, for he wakes "In the moon that is always rising" (the night which now will always be there), and he discovers that the farm has "forever fled from the childless land." In this way the theme of joy and loss; that is, of the transience of childhood's joy, is brought to completion.

In a similar fashion, the theme of transfiguration functions in the liturgy—as framing, and as rhythmic and cumulative repetition with variations. In its statement—or rather in its actual working out of man's transformation—different means are employed. This takes place in somewhat the same way as we have seen, in music, the different instruments play the lead in the separate movements, or as in literature different symbols serve to present the poetic theme.

2. *Transfiguration: what it is, its effects*

"Fern Hill," as we have seen, says that a child may be happy for a while—time tolerates his joy—but soon innocence and happiness will vanish. This is the theme of the poem. It is presented in many different ways.

The liturgy, for its theme, says in countless ways that God, using created instruments, transfigures man. God ennobles man and gives him joy by sharing with him his own divine life. He does this by using things perceptible to man's senses.

In this process man and things are changed and God is given glory.

Even purely material things undergo a change: they are hallowed and then shown to us as possessed of new value, new beauty. Man, too, is changed. He is transformed because God's grace and power flood his being. Then as the culmination of these two hallowings, transfigured man, using the things of God's transfigured world, is empowered to praise God effectively and to offer him gifts which please him.

Transfiguration, then, is a hallowing of men and of things that they in turn may glorify God. The liturgy is the point of contact where natural and supernatural worlds meet in a special way. And when they meet in order to effect this transfiguration, all the resources of spiritual and material words are called into play. This is so because the transformation of man is accomplished "through sacrifice and sacrament and prayer, that is, through the liturgy." [27]

Involved here, as we can see, are three beings: God, man, and the things of the natural world. Accordingly, the liturgy's transfiguring work has three effects. First, because of their hallowing, and their use by God, things are newly revealed to us—they undergo an epiphany. This effect takes place largely on the natural level. Such a revelation of the nobility in things we shall call an *epiphanal* tendency of transfiguration.

Besides this, there are two purely supernatural happenings which result from transfiguration. In one case, God's power, working through things, floods down on man. This is the *sacramental* effect of the liturgy. And finally, man is empowered to offer gifts to God. He offers Christ under the appearances of bread and wine; he offers himself, frequently using symbols to signify his self-offering; he offers creation to God by giving it voice to praise him. All these are aspects of the *sacrificial* tendency of transfiguration in the liturgy.

These words, *sacramental* and *sacrificial*, have in theology a highly exact and specialized meaning, but here we are using them in the widest possible sense. By sacrificial we mean the empowering of things, through the liturgy, with the ability to become gifts offered to God's glory. A sacrifice in this nontechnical sense, may be any gift presented to God—from the unique and excelling sacrifice of the Mass, to the praise God receives whenever a Christian recites a psalm. This last is a way of lending words to the inarticulate creation. By such praying we lift up to God:

> sun and moon ... every star that shines ...
> monsters of the sea and all its depths;
> fire and hail, snow and ice, and the storm
>   wind that executes his decree. ...
> All mountains and hills, all ... fruit trees
>   and cedars   (Psalm 148).

Sacrifice is, therefore, an upward, Godward gesture. This lifting up of earthly things to God is the sacrificial aspect of transfiguration.

Then further, by the sacramental effect of transfiguration, we mean that through God's action things are invested with power to bring grace to man. The sacramental effect is, therefore, a downward, manward, movement from God towards human beings. At the end of this chapter we shall present some concrete examples of these sacrificial, sacramental, and epiphanal effects of God's hallowing power. And these ideas will be basic to the last four chapters of the book. Before we proceed, however, it would be well to clarify further the epiphanal tendency of the liturgy, since this one is not so commonly spoken of as are the other two effects.

We have said that the liturgy furnishes, even on the natural level, an epiphany, a revelation. For one thing, the hallowing and ennobling of creation in the liturgy directs our attention to these things. Then again, the Church re-shapes things according to her own determination, as an artist does. She imposes form on them; she places them in a new context, and she shows them to us as effective on a level higher than their simple natural one.

In this way she not only reveals God to us by means of them, she not only teaches us supernatural truths by her use of them, but she also calls our attention to their natural qualities. Her use of them, therefore, functions as art does, because both art and the liturgy render visible to us new aspects of creation. By this kind of revelation we are encouraged to look with new eyes at these treasures of the natural world, to see them in a new way. This idea was mentioned earlier, in our discussion of the variety found in creation. It is now time to discuss it in more detail.

We might compare this revelation with the change of outlook which the great French painter, Cezanne, brought to those who look at paintings. In his time, the impressionists were attempting to represent the appearance of light on surfaces. But Cezanne decided that the form of the object was more important than the accidental light, which was subject to change. The form, he thought, was always there. And so he painted apples that look so solid we think they might have been modelled in clay.

Cezanne said, too, that all forms, everything in nature, could be reduced to simple geometric solids. This is one way of saying that a tree trunk is a cylinder; a house is a cube with a triangular prism for a roof, that under the surface of the apple is a sphere, and a mountain reduced to its lowest terms is a cone or a pyramid. This awareness of the solid reality under things gave Cezanne's apples and mountains a new appearance of solidity. He saw them from a new point of view and painted them in a new way. In doing this he shattered our accustomed way of seeing things, and gave us new glasses with which to look at them. Now we see mountains and apples as Cezanne the artist revealed them to us.

There is an old Chinese saying which insists that what the artist tries to show us is not only the tiger, but the very "tigerness of the tiger." The same thing was said in different words by the man who remarked that "art does not render the visible; it renders visible." In other words, the artist's aim is not to show us things we already see quite clearly—not to render the already visible—but to *render visible* to our eyes and minds some aspect of an object, a person, which was there all the time, but was invisible to us until the artist pointed it out.

In this way the artist shares his vision with us, and we find ourselves saying, "Of course mountains look like this, but until now I never saw them so."

On an analogous, but higher level, is that which happened during the transfiguration of our Lord on Mount Thabor (Matt. 17). It can serve as an example of God's way of making something visible which had not been seen before.

St. Matthew says that one day Christ led three of his apostles up to a high mountain. "And he was transfigured in their presence, his face shining like the sun, and his garments becoming white as snow. . . . And now there was a voice . . . This is my beloved Son, in whom I am well pleased; to him, then, listen." At this, the apostles were terrified and fell on their faces.

But after a little while Jesus came near, and in his old friendly way he touched them, "Arise, he said, do not be afraid." And they lifted up their eyes and saw "no man there but Jesus only." Their everyday friend, with whom they had eaten and argued and trudged dusty roads, was near them again. They heard the familiar words which were almost a motto of his: "Do not be afraid." They looked up and saw once more "no man there but Jesus only." "Only the carpenter of Nazareth," as Archbishop Goodier puts it with loving irony, "only the Son of the living God!" [28]

In this incident we find that the divinity of Christ, which

all his life he had kept hidden, was allowed to overflow its bounds and flood even his human body with glory. Until this time he had appeared to be a very ordinary person. We remember that his neighbors could not believe that he would do anything unusual. At one time they showed their opinion of him by saying: "Is not this the carpenter's son, whose mother is called Mary.... How is it that all this has come to him?" (Matt. 14:55-56). Now this "carpenter of Nazareth" is seen to become "shining like the sun" (Matt. 17:2). His garments become "bright... white as no fuller here on earth could have made them" (Mark 9:2). His humanity was transfigured, and there was an epiphany, a revelation of his divine power and glory.

The apostles, when they saw him, fell down in fear. They were paralyzed by the sight, for as T. S. Eliot says, "Humankind cannot bear very much reality." We know that it is especially hard for us human beings to bear divine reality, therefore God does not often reveal himself so directly as he does here in Christ's transfiguration. Usually he shows his glory in oblique fashion—veiled in materials which are used as sacramental signs and symbols. Through them he manifests his significance and his power.

Always after this day, the apostles must have been seeing under the appearance of "the carpenter of Nazareth," the deeper reality—the glory of the "Son of the living God." In a certain sense we might say that the humanity of Christ functioned here like a sacrament—it "brought God within our reach," within the grasp of the apostles' senses.

Once in a while, through the liturgy's epiphanal power, we too catch some glimpse of God's glory hidden under material veils. When we are so allowed some insight which shows us human and material reality as endowed with divine significance and power we are flooded with joy. But like the apostles, we too "cannot bear very much reality." And so, like the apostles after the transfiguration, we must come down from the mountain of vision to our daily world.

This means that we cannot always hold our moments of insight—those times when the opacity of things has become transparent. Nevertheless such a vision has permanent effects. The opaque glass of surface appearances has been shattered, and the hidden reality beneath it has been revealed.

The glass of appearance may be replaced. And the replacement may not be completely transparent. But from now on the surface of things will be at least translucent. It will allow the reality to shine through. From this time on we will be permanently conscious that divinity is at work above the winds, under our feet.

3. *Transfiguration: the purpose of Christianity*

This hallowing and transfiguration of man and of the world, for the glory of God, is the purpose of the Christian religion. As Dom Herwegen puts it: Christianity exists "to assume man to God through Christ . . . to bring us as transfigured Christians to the transfigured Christ."

Frequently we find Christ himself stating this theme. He often says that he has come to transform things. He tells us, "I have come that they may have life, and have it more abundantly" (John 10:10). "The water I give . . . will be a spring . . . within [a man], that flows continually to bring him everlasting life" (John 4:14). "It is fire that I have come to spread over the earth, and what better wish can I have than that it should be kindled?" (Luke 12:49). What is born by natural birth is a thing of nature, what is born by spiritual birth is a thing of spirit. . . . The wind breathes where it will . . . so it is, when a man is born by the breath of the Spirit" (John 3:6-8).

Again, St. Peter insists on this newness, this transfiguration, this investiture with a different life: "You are children new-born, and all your craving must be for the soul's pure milk, that will nurture you into salvation . . . you have tasted . . . the goodness of the Lord. Draw near to him . . . you . . . must be built upon him, stones that live and breathe, into a spiritual fabric; you must be a holy priesthood to offer up that spiritual sacrifice which God accepts through Jesus Christ" (I Peter 2:2-5). Here St. Peter employs many metaphors to convey his meaning: the Christians are "children new-born"; they are a new building; they are a holy priesthood newly prepared to offer sacrifice to God.

St. Paul also, in his own way tells how the coming of Christ has begun a transformation which can be seen in everything. His epistle to the Hebrews is one example. Here the key word is *better*. He tells the chosen people that the Old Covenant, the agreement that God made with his people, was good. But the New Covenant in Christ is better—it is the fulfillment of the former. Moses was a true follower of God, but Christ is better—he is God's own Son. The priesthood of the old law was a holy thing, but the priesthood of Christ is a better reality. It is the reality of which the levitical priesthood was only a shadow.

The first object of this Christian transfiguration is, of course, always the human being. God "has destined [us] to be moulded into the image of his Son" (Romans 8:29). We are to be shaped to the likeness of Christ. We are to become images—imitations—of Christ. Each of us is a copy of him, but like works of art, each one is to image Christ in a highly individualized way.

Just as we might have a dozen pictures of the same sunset, painted by a dozen different artists, and every picture would be different, so a countless number of human beings can imitate Christ, can be transformed into him through the power of the sacraments, and each portrayal will be different. They will differ according to the materials (individual personality, circumstances of each life) used. They will vary according to the vantage point from which each individual views Christ, the interpretation he puts upon the actions of God-made-visible in Christ, the degree of his receptivity to the graces offered him. Each one, in other words, will portray different traits of Christ, and to a different degree.

Christians are transformed by coming to union with Christ in many ways. They share his joy: "So that my joy may be theirs, and reach its full measure in them" (John 17:13). They share his oneness with the Father: "That they too may be one in us, as thou Father, art in me, and I in thee . . . that while thou art in me, I may be in them" (John 17:21-23). They share the Father's own love for Christ. When the Father looks on Christ's followers, he in some way sees in them his beloved Son in whom he is well pleased: "so that the love thou hast bestowed upon me may dwell in them" (John 17:26). Finally, the Christian lives with Christ's very life, "so that . . . I, too, may dwell in them" (John 17:26), says our Lord.

In all these ways the documents of Christianity bear witness to the transfiguration of man. But man is not alone in being transformed. Nature also shares in the sacramental, sacrificial, and epiphanal effects of transfiguration. Let us, for a moment, think especially about this last—the epiphany which results from God's use of things. This revelation of natural qualities is characteristic of Christ's own mode of procedure during his life on earth.

For example, what Christian, familiar with the New Testament, can see a hen spreading her wings to shelter her chicks, and not remember the wonderful comparison used by our Lord to describe his love for us: "How often have I been ready to gather thy children together, as a hen gathers her chickens under her wings" (Matt. 23:37). Who but God would think of showing us divine love under the appearance of such a thing as a mother bird. And does not the comparison cause us to look with fresh vision even at clucking mother hens?

Then again, when in our explorings, we come upon a mountain valley filled with poppies, are we not tempted to say, again in Christ's words: "Why should you be anxious over clothing? See how the wild lilies grow; they do not toil or spin; and yet I tell you that even Solomon in all his glory was not arrayed like one of these" (Matt. 6:28).

It is said that the poet's best gift is the ability to make good metaphors—to see likenesses between apparently unlike things, and show them to us. If we read the New Testament with this thought in mind, we shall see in what a masterly fashion Christ uses metaphors to teach his sublime lessons: You are of more value than sparrows; you are like the wild lilies—your Father cares for you. The kingdom of heaven is like a pearl; it is priceless. God's kingdom is like a net cast into the sea (inclusive, all-embracing), like yeast in dough (making the weight of our selfishness light, disappearing as yeast does when its work is finished). No wonder men said of him: "Nobody has ever spoken as this man speaks" (John 7:46). Again and again, Christ transfigures ordinary things in this extraordinary way.

Another kind of transfiguration can be seen in the way our Lord built the Lord's Prayer from older phrases, doing what the poet does when he places well-worn words in new contexts to sharpen their meaning. The phrases, "Hallowed be thy name; thy kingdom come," were, for example, not something entirely new, entirely foreign to accustomed thought. The words were familiar to the apostles because they belonged to the commonly used Jewish prayer of thanksgiving, the Kaddish, which is still prayed today: "May the great *name of God be exalted* and sanctified in the world which he created *according to his will,* and may he cause his *kingdom to come* in your lives and in your days. . . ."

The frequent use of this prayer had, perhaps, taken away

the vividness of their impact, worn its phrases smooth, as a coin through handling loses its sharp imprint. But Christ renewed men's awareness of their meaning by placing the words in a new context, and especially by introducing the familiar phrases with the startlingly new words, "Our Father." After thus focusing men's attention, he went on with the well known petitions for the glory of God's name ("hallowed be thy name"), the coming of his kingdom ("thy kingdom come"), and the doing of his will ("thy will be done").

In doing this, Christ, particularly by the introductory phrase, "Our Father," added a new dimension of meaning to all the words of the prayer, and gave them a new power in God's sight. The poet, Péguy, puts the description of this transfiguration in the voice of the Father himself, who says in the poem:

> *Our Father who art in heaven,* my son taught them that prayer. . . .
> He knew very well what he was doing that day, my son who loved them so.
> When he put that barrier between them and me,
>   *Our Father who art in heaven*
>   Those three or four words.
> That barrier which my anger and perhaps my justice will never pass. . . .
>
> And now I must judge them like a father. As if a father were any good as a judge.
>   *A certain man had two sons.* . . .[29]

By using the words *Our Father,* therefore, to begin his prayer, our Lord gave a new significance and a new power to its phrases. Hearing this introduction, the eternal Father looks at the words of the prayer with different eyes. He becomes unable to resist their power. They are rendered visible, even to him, in a new way. They become sacrificial gifts offered to God—sacramental realities able to channel God's graces to man.

The poet shows that Christ transfigured all of prayer by the words *Our Father,* for with these words he poured a new light on our relationship with God by naming him Father. By these means the Father is constrained to listen and have mercy ("and now I must judge them like a father").

In these ways and in many others, we can see that the coming of Christ, his life in his historical body in Palestine, and his life in his mystical body in America and Italy and Australia in our twentieth century, is a change from the old way of the world. It is a betterment, a transformation, a transfiguration.

Such transfiguration reveals new beauty in nature. Moreover, it lifts up all things: stars and water, fruits and beasts, the coolness and the destructive power of winds—to a new level of sacrificial value, making of them gifts which man can offer to God, gifts which are pleasing to God.

Then after these gifts are offered to God, they are received back by man. And now they are given sacramental effectiveness. By this power they serve as instruments in the hand of Christ. Through them he bestows on man that share in God's life which we call grace. In this way he works an inward transformation in man.

4. *Transfiguration at work in the liturgy*

In a certain sense, transfiguration might be described as an invasion of the natural by the supernatural. The liturgy is never a purely mental or spiritual thing. We might compare it to man himself and say that it has, like him, a body and a soul. For one thing, there is always present some element which appeals to the senses: words or music which can be spoken and heard, bread and wine which can be eaten and drunk, oil and water and fire which affect our sense of touch, acts and gestures which employ our sense of motion, the fragrances of incense and of balsam which please our sense of smell. These we might call the "body" of the liturgy. Such are the instruments God uses for his transfiguring purposes.

These natural instruments (words, acts, materials, events) are, moreover, transformed. They are invested with spiritual power. For "God wished to make not only spiritual, but material nature His temple and through the Holy Spirit to admit this temple to a participation in a supernatural sanctity and glory." [30]

Now one thing we notice is that the depth of this invasion of the natural by the supernatural varies widely. Things are more or less consecrated, more or less hallowed. This hallowing is deepest in the Mass, where bread and wine lose their proper substances and are transubstantiated, so that the true and living substance of Christ's body and blood become present. In other cases the change is not so radical.

For example, there are various consecrations and blessings which sanctify, but do not change the substance of things. The holy oils destined for use in the sacraments present an instance of a very powerful consecration, which is, however, not comparable to that which happens in the Mass. There is, nevertheless, a real penetration of the material thing by the holiness of God, as can be seen in the following prayer: [31]

> From this oil keep thy distance [foul fiend], and let it be a spiritual salve . . . to the strengthening of men's bodies, that are temples of the living God. Make room for the Holy Spirit to dwell here . . . in the name of God . . .

The last phrase, in particular, shows God's "invasion," in the words: "Make room for the Holy Spirit to dwell here."

In the next selection from the same blessing we see this idea reiterated, and the significances of anointing are pointed out to us:

Hallow [the richness of this substance] with thy blessing. *Charge it with the power* of the Holy Spirit, the grace of Christ thy Son thereto aiding; from his name Chrism we learned to call it, when priest and king, prophet and martyr, should receive thy unction.[32]

Here we discover that the holy oils receive a new name (Chrism) fashioned on Christ's name. We also learn that the person anointed is to receive in mysterious ways the powers of priest and king, prophet and martyr. By his anointing with these hallowed oils he is given the right and duty to worship God and to offer the Mass along with the fully ordained priest. He also shares in the qualities of king, prophet, and martyr: rule or control over himself, truthfulness and zeal in spreading God's word, courage to bear sufferings for the kingdom of God.

A less solemn blessing is that invoked on water. In it we find, however, that the water like the consecrated oil, is charged with a power which is beyond its purely natural capacity. Here is the blessing for our commonly used holy water:

O God, who for the welfare of mankind has made use of the substance of water as a vehicle of so many . . . graces, listen kindly . . . and impart . . . thy blessing to this element. . . . Let this water, created by thee and destined for use in the sacred liturgy, acquire the efficacy of divine grace. . . .

May anything that threatens the safety or peace of those who dwell [where it shall have been sprinkled] come to nothing.[33]

In this manner, holy water is made a vehicle of God's grace, and is invested with a blessing which is intended to protect the homes of men from anything that threatens their safety or peace.

Still other blessings are bestowed on fields and food, on tools and bells and buildings. And finally, there is the informal blessing which comes to these inarticulate things when they are absorbed into man's willed and formulated praise of God, for instance in the psalms.

That there are differences in degree in these transformations can be seen even more clearly in the greater or less degree of ceremony with which these blessed and consecrated things are handled.

The Eucharist, for example, is to be touched only by the consecrated hands of the priest, and with the greatest possible reverence. This care extends even to the vessels and linens used in connection with it.

The holy oils are treated with nearly as great ceremony, while on the other hand, holy water is used in all kinds of circumstances by all kinds of people. It is, nevertheless, still something set aside, something differentiated from ordinary water. Fields and food, tools and ships, however, when they are blessed are not at all set aside from daily life. They continue to be used and enjoyed freely by human beings in ordinary living.

Now before concluding this chapter on transfiguration and its epiphanal, sacrificial, and sacramental effects, let us analyze two prayers which present these three effects to us. The first is from the Preface for the Mass of Christmastide:

> Right indeed it is and just, proper and for our welfare, that we should always and everywhere give thanks ... for through the *mystery of the Word made flesh thy splendour* has shone before our mind's eye with *a new radiance,* and through him whom we recognize as *God made visible* we are carried away in love of *things invisible.* . . .
> (Sheed and Ward Missal, italics added).

Here the Church says that God's glory, his splendor, has shone before our eyes because the Word was made flesh. His coming has showed us a new radiance of the divinity. If we ponder these words we discover that with the Incarnation we have received a revelation of the glory of God—this is the main import of the prayer.

And this revelation is emphasized in the next phrase: "Through him . . . we recognize God made visible"; that is, we see the invisible God taking to himself a human visible body, and so making it possible for our senses to grasp him.

Then immediately the Church prays that this revelation of the radiant glory of God may act with sacramental power to bring God's grace to us—that it may work an inner change in us. She prays that the sight of divinity revealed in Christ may "carry us away in love of things invisible." Then when we are thus carried away into a selfless love, our very love itself becomes a sacrificial gift to God.

The secret prayer for the second Mass at Christmas presents the three phases of transfiguration even more forcibly. Here is the prayer:

> As this day's new born human child shone with the brightness of the Godhead, so may the earthly substance of this offering bring the divine within our reach.

The first phrase of this prayer is epiphanal. It shows us how the revelation of God comes about. It says that the new born human child shines "with the brightness of the Godhead." Hidden under his human helplessness is all power and all glory. Then looking at him, knowing the truth about him, we find the "brightness of the Godhead" becoming visible to us. In him we have "sight of his glory, glory such as belongs to the Father's only-begotten Son" (John 1:14).

A sacrificial or gift-giving aspect of the mystery is present as well as this epiphanal one. It appears in the words which here describe both the mystery of the incarnation and the Mass immediately in progress. Both of these realities are referred to in the phrase, "the earthly substance of this offering." This offering is first of all the earthly substance of

Christ's humanity united in the incarnation to his divinity in order that he may become humankind's gift to God.

And second, the earthly substance is the bread and wine we offer, which will, in the Mass, be transubstantiated. By this act, it will become that Christ who is lifted up to the Father by the hands of the priest. Such is the sacrificial meaning of the prayer.

The last phrase, finally, expresses the sacramental function of both incarnation and Mass. It says, "May the earthly substance of this offering *bring the divine within our reach.*" That is, may the gift we have offered, of our humanity, of our bread and wine, now changed into thy Son, make it possible for us to come into contact with him. May it literally bring the divine within our grasp. May we reach out and take hold of God and keep him for our possession.

The theme of transfiguration in Christianity, and especially in the liturgy, then, operates in a sacrificial, a sacramental, and an epiphanal way. By such transfiguring action the "world is charged with the grandeur of God" (as Hopkins says), so that all things can bring him within our reach, and so that we in turn may be lifted into ever-increasing union with him.

All these events come about through Christ our Lord, as the Church insists. And from him, who is the center of the liturgy's circles, transformation goes out like the widening circles from a stone dropped in water. As this happens, the whole universe is given voice to sing the *Gloria,* to exult with Christ's own praise of the Father, and man and all the things in the world cry out: "We give thee thanks for thy great glory."

To catch even a passing glimpse of these great realities is to perceive that "transfiguration is the art-principle of the liturgy." This is to discover a wider Christian joy and an expanded awareness of the areas for delight in the Christian life.

Now one of the techniques which Christ and his Church employ to bring about this transformation is the use of symbols, especially those related to earth, air, fire, and water. In the next chapter, therefore, we shall treat of man's need for symbols, the meaning of symbolism, and the particular qualities and functions of the symbols related to the four elements of earth, air, fire, and water.

CHAPTER FOUR

Of Symbols and the Four Elements

> ... I cry with tumbledown tongue,
> Count my blessings aloud:
> Four elements and five
> Senses, and man a spirit in love
> Tangling through this spun slime
> To his nimbus bell cool kingdom come. . . .
>
> The whole world then. . . .
> Spins its morning of praise.
>
> DYLAN THOMAS [34]

SOME OF GOD'S DELIGHT in his creation, a jubilation added to our natural vision, comes when we discover that the world we live in is a transfigured world—that Christianty's whole purpose is one of transfiguration. Then we know that creation, like Mary in Hopkins' poem to her, "This one work has to do—Let all God's glory through." [35]

When this insight comes, creation itself stands revealed in beauty—rendered visible to us in all its rich variety and serene unity. We also see that nature is given new significance and power—a power which functions sacrificially to lift praise to the majesty of God, and sacramentally to channel the life of God to us.

Now one of the important ways that this glory is shown to us, and this power is rendered effective, is through symbols.

God's transforming action, in other words, affects us through the things we see and hear and touch.

When Gerard Manley Hopkins said, "The world is charged with the grandeur of God," [36] he said well. And the psalmist says better: "Glory and beauty are thy clothing. The light is a garment thou dost wrap about thee ... on the wings of the wind thou dost come and go" (Ps. 103:2).

Because "the earth is the Lord's" (Ps. 23:1), therefore "Thrills the barren desert with rejoicing; the wilderness takes heart and blossoms, fair as the lily. Blossom on blossom, it will rejoice and sing" for it "shall see the glory of the Lord" (Isaias 35:1-2). God's glory shines out from the world, as the divinity shone forth from Christ's human person during his transfiguration—though, of course, he was a divine person, while the world only glows with reflected glory. One of the ways in which this hidden glory gleams out to us is through symbols.

1. *The need for symbols*

The need to be aware of the material elements around us, to be in actual touch with them, is deeply rooted in our very humanity. We need not only to use them, to exploit them for our purely utilitarian ends, but also to reverence them as beings full of wonder in themselves, and as signs pointing to realities beyond themselves. In a sacramental and sacrificial universe, moreover, they function beyond beauty; they become channels for contact to be made between God and man.

We need symbols to renew our union with nature and to keep us in touch with her. We need to recover our delight in fire and vines, food and candles, oil and the shelter of palms. Unless we stop now and then and look at them, we may in our daily hurry lose sight of these natural treasures. But what is even more important, we need symbols because they help to effect, especially through the liturgy, our union with God. For it is through the use of symbols, especially the four basic natural symbols of earth, air, fire, and water, that God effects his sacrificial and sacramental purpose of bringing man to union with him.

By the use of these symbols, Christ and his Church incorporate us in the life of grace—bring us new life, and increase our created sharing in the divine life. A living awareness of these things can revitalize our relationships with the world, each other, and God. As Father Barden, the Irish theologian, has said: "In modern man's isolation and loneliness he hungers for life and wholeness, and it is this hunger which the symbol heals."

Like a recurring theme the warning rings out in our day against the loss of awareness of our roots in nature, and the consequent impoverishment of the life of the spirit. The recovery of this awareness is one service that can be done for us by the artistry of human beings and the artistry of God in the liturgy. For, as we have said, art renders newly visible to us these elemental realities which are ours by right of heritage.

The danger of such a loss is of deep concern to writers of our time from Karl Jung, the psychiatrist and psychologist, to T. S. Eliot, the poet, from Father Vann, the teacher, to Suzanne Langer, the philosopher of aesthetics.

Father Vann says that ours is a "cellophane age" in which man at times insulates himself from life, because life means change, growth, and therefore discomfort. We need to guard ourselves lest we become like Eliot's *Waste Land* dwellers who say:

> April is the cruellest month, breeding
> Lilacs out of the dead land . . . stirring
> Dull roots with rain.
> Winter kept us warm, covering
> Earth in forgetful snow.

Unless we are alert, we can become like those who would rather be dead, "covered in forgetful snow," than alive like spring-time earth. We run the danger of becoming like Eliot's women of Canterbury (in *Murder in the Cathedral*) who "fear disturbance of the seasons" when "ruinous spring shall beat at the doors." [37]

Like them, we do not want to be forced from our comfortable apathy. Sometimes surrounded by luxuries, we would rather be half-living than suffer inconvenience ("winter kept us warm"). We do not want any kind of new life ("breeding lilacs out of the dead land") because it entails the sacrifice of our lethargy.

To guard against such dulling of delight in natural things, we need a renewed awareness of the beauty and significance in and behind the elements of nature which are needed for life—the meanings of water and the cycle of seasons, the rhythm of alternating light and dark in which "each echoes its secret to the next, each night passes on its revelation of knowledge" (Ps. 18:3).

These things are of value in themselves for their wonderful variety. And their use in the liturgy endows them with new significance and new unity. Besides this, they function as instruments for God's transfiguring action, because God's power affects us through things our senses perceive.

2. *What symbols are*

Symbols are material things, things we taste or see or touch, used to signify something other than themselves—some reality lying on a deeper or higher level than the purely material. They signify realities either too big to be thought about comfortably, or too mysterious for the mind to grapple with directly.

Think, for example, of one such symbol—a material thing, a bird—which stands for the attractive and complex idea of freedom. Thousands of times men have asked themselves, Can I not "escape, like a frightened sparrow, to the hill-side?" (Ps. 10:2). They have watched the swift flight of birds and envied them. Because the bird flies effortlessly into the mysterious blue space where we cannot follow, it makes us think of escape from hampering duty or our own inertia—of freedom from all that holds us down to earth.

In the opera *I Pagliacci,* Nedda sings a lovely song which expresses this universal idea. She is burdened by her "restless heart," and suddenly, looking up, she sees the birds "like arrows of light in the sky":

> No night dismays them, no storm delays them. . . .
> For they fly on wings untiring,
> Seeking sweet regions they may never know,
> For what can bar their dreams and their desiring?

The psalmist, too, employs the same symbol, when he says: "Trembling and terrified, I watched the darkness closing about me. Had I but wings, I cry, as a dove has wings, to fly away and find rest! How distant would my journey be . . . out in the wilderness!" (Ps. 54:6-8).

When we think in this way, the bird becomes something more than a bird in its significance. It becomes a symbol—a thing existing on the material level of being (a bird made of bones and flesh and feathers), and at the same time pointing to a higher, non-material, level of meaning (the concept of freedom).

Another obvious example of symbolism is the flag of one's country. It is something we can see and touch. It is red, white, and blue cloth waving in the wind. In itself it forms an interesting and vivid pattern of color against the sky. But more than this, because it has been chosen by men to symbolize a certain country, it suggests a whole complex of ideas and feelings connected with one's own country: home and heroes, weather and landscape, pride in her past and concern for her future. The flag is, then, another kind of symbol, an arbitrary one, whose meaning has been given to it by man's choice. The bird, on the other hand, is what we call a natural symbol, standing for freedom in every country and every age.

Many descriptions and attempts at definitions of symbols have been offered by thoughtful persons. It may be enlightening to look at a few of them.

Suzanne Langer, a noted philosopher, in her book, *Feeling and Form*, says that "a symbol is used to articulate ideas of something we wish to think about, and until we have a fairly adequate symbolism we cannot think about it." [38] The symbol, then, is a language of the mind, a *word* in concrete form, which we need in order to articulate our thoughts to ourselves.

Such a description, it is true, applies equally well to the use of symbols by mathematicians and scientists, and to their very different use by artists of all kinds, including those who have shaped the great poetry of worship.

A mathematician or a scientist uses symbols in a certain way. He wants his symbols to be as pure, as sterile, as singular in reference as possible. His *one* should equal *one*, an abstraction, and it should call nothing else to mind: neither one tall palm, nor one colored bouncing ball, nor one chord of music.

The scientist, in other words, wants his symbols to be purely denotative. He would like to strip them of all rich but disorderly connotations. He says that water is H_2O, and he is annoyed if his abstract reasonings are intruded upon by thoughts of cold showers needling his shoulders, of sluggish irrigation canals, or of Yosemite's Bridal Veil waterfall.

The poet and the man of prayer, however, use symbols differently. They wish their symbols to include a rich and complex reference to reality. Water, for example, might mean the lassitude of Tennyson's lotos eaters adrift on strange seas with all desire for home dead in them. It might mean the deceptive blue of an ocean where Moby Dick, the malignant white whale lurks. Again, it might tempt one to be silent, as the poet Auden suggests, "That through the channels of the ear/ May wander like a river/ The swaying sound of the sea."

To the man of prayer, the thought of water may bring to mind the longing poetry of Advent: "Send down dew you heavens, and let the skies pour down upon us the rain we long for, him, the just one: may he, the Saviour, spring from the closed womb of the earth" (Introit, Fourth Sunday of Advent). Or again, water may suggest Christ's quieting the storm on the lake, or his standing in line at the Jordan waiting for John to baptize him.

It might even happen that all these meanings and more could be simultaneously present to the mind of one thinking as an artist thinks. For artists and men of prayer both practice a contemplative kind of thought—a circling, serene, and inclusive gaze at things. Because of this they value their symbols not for specific reference to a definite quality or quantity, but for their multi-levelled meanings.

Both the scientist's and the artist's mode of thought and expression are necessary to man. Accurate scientific knowledge is needed not only in regard to material things, but even in reasoning about God, as the clear and organized discussions in philosophy and theology textbooks show.

But knowledge through art-symbols gives a different insight. "A symbol," Father Bede Griffiths quotes Goethe as saying, "is a revelation of the unfathomable in a moment of life." It reveals a meaning on a deeper level (unfathomable) by means of a concrete thing perceptible to the senses (in a moment of life). This moment of life, this experience or object which our senses can catch hold of, acts as a pointer to something other, something mysterious, to the unfathomable which we cannot think about without some concrete thing on which we can focus our thoughts.

Even more appropriate for our present discussion is the definition of Dr. Karl Jung. He says that "the symbolic process is an experience *in the image and of the image*." [39] He is saying, for the purpose of describing a psychological process, that in using symbols we have two experiences. One is on the sense level: we see, hear, feel, smell, taste such things as food, trees, fire, springtime, winter. Here our experience is *of the image* itself. We taste the crusty crispness of bread, or its tough resilience. We see the slenderness of the tree or the wide spread of its branches. We feel invigorated with spring or apathetic from cold.

But also we have a second experience. The concrete thing or event points to a further level of meaning. Here we have an experience *in the image*. For instance, food means home and security; or implicit in one tree's slenderness which sways in the wind, may be a meaning of carefree gaiety; or the spreading branches of a fig tree may suggest that it would be easily climbed—children might like to hide among its leaves. This last thought, in turn, may make one think of someone beloved who stretches wide arms in welcome. Again, the wood of the tree may remind us of the "sweet wood" (in the Good Friday phrase) of Christ's saving cross. All these meanings are experiences in the image.

We receive, therefore, in symbols, an experience of the image, by means of which we see, touch, smell, some thing or event. And we enter into another meaning, have another experience, through and in the image. By means of this second experience, we know something more profound and complex than mere sense experience.

From the above discussion, we see that there are three aspects to symbolism. First, in our seeing beyond the symbol into a deeper reality, we do not lose the symbol itself. We admire the actual wetness of the rain even while we pray that the "skies [may] pour down upon us the rain we long for, him, the . . . Saviour" (Introit, Fourth Sun. Advent).

Second, the symbol points to another reality. It *is* a material thing and remains a material thing, but it *means* also a spiritual or intellectual thing. The bird means freedom. The flag means patriotism.

Third, this reference to something on a higher level does not consist in one single, simple meaning, but is made up of a complex of meanings. Take the idea of freedom, or of patriotism, for example. If we asked five of our friends to discuss either of them, would we not get a variety of ideas connected with these concepts?

To clarify these three points, let us take the common symbol of the lamb which refers to Christ. The lamb, firstly, is an ordinary little animal, not rare or strikingly beautiful. Secondly, it is gentle—we think of it as characterized by patience. And thirdly, the lamb furnishes meat which can be eaten.

With these natural references in mind we see many meanings behind the speech of St. John the Baptist when he pointed to Christ and said, "Behold the Lamb of God" (or in another translation), "Look, this is the Lamb of God" (John 1:29 and 1:36). We realize among other things, how ordinary the Son of God allowed himself to appear that day when he, the carpenter, walked along the banks of the Jordan and John pointed him out to Andrew.

Perhaps we also think of the prophecy of Isaias (53:6-7): "We were all strayed sheep, each following his own path, and the guilt that belonged to all of us God has laid on him. . . . He might be a sheep that is being led away to the slaughter house, a lamb standing there dumb while it is shorn." And we remember that in his passion, Christ, like a lamb, allowed himself to be shorn, to be stripped of his clothes before the crucifixion. Like the lamb, he accepted each event. He resisted no attack.

Finally, we may think of the sacrifice of the paschal lamb in the Old Testament—that lamb whose blood saved God's people, and whose flesh was eaten at a ceremonial meal. Thinking these thoughts we may come at last to the remembrance of our paschal sacrifice and our paschal meal at the Mass, wherein we pray, "Lamb of God, who takes away the sins of the world, have mercy on us . . . grant us peace."

3. *The four elements as symbols*

Probably the most basic symbols of all are those of earth, air, fire, and water, and the things related to them. Ancient peoples believed that these were the constituents of everything in the universe. And as we know, they are still important and even necessary for man's life.

Each of these elements has a destructive and a constructive aspect. Earth supports by its solidity, and nourishes by its fruits, but it also threatens by earthquakes. Out of its substance things grow, and to it the dead return. Air can be a destroying whirlwind or a sustaining breath. Fire ravages, but it also warms and heals. Water cleanses and refreshes, but its floods sweep away the lives and works of man.

Looking at these elements in another way, we can say that each influences man's environment and each supports his life. From these natural meanings certain natural symbols arise. We will here limit our discussion to two kinds of significance for each element.

From this point of view, we have two concepts about earth: extension in space (which affects man's environment particularly), and fruitfulness (which supports his life). The former suggests mountains and deserts and all land contours, also dwellings and shelters on earth's surface. It further calls up the thought of journeys across the miles of earth (and the symbol of man's life as a journey is an ancient and omnipresent one). The latter concept, that of fruitfulness, gives us symbols taken from such things as food and clothing, and all kinds of planting, growth, fructifying, and death.

Air manifests itself in two main ways: in winds which affect climate and change our environment, and in the breath we draw to sustain our life. Fire also has two main qualities: light and heat. Light makes a great difference in man's environment. Think of the contrast between the life of an Eskimo in his long dark winter, and that of the people in other lands.

Fire, too, protects man from dangers in a wild environment. How many men in the wilderness have been kept safe from savage animals by firelight. Heat can destroy life, but it can also preserve man from cold, and comfort him psychologically (think of the family happiness around a fireplace).

Water also has two main effects: it cleanses and it causes things to live and grow. Both of these significances are important, for example, in the sacrament of baptism. These natural meanings form the basis for very much natural symbolism, as we shall see.

All the natural symbols and their rich meanings are used by Christ to signify and effect supernatural meanings and transformations. Since we now have some orderly idea of the four elements and their symbolism, we are ready to see how they function in the circles of the liturgy. First, however, we shall consider Christ as the center of the system of worship called the liturgy. After that we shall take in turn the circles of the Mass, the sacraments, the office, and the year.

TRANSITION

CHAPTER FIVE

Of Christ the Center

> All things find in him their origin,
> their impulse, the center of their
> being; to him be glory (Rom. 11:36)
>
> I saw God in a Point . . . by which sight
> I saw that He is in all things . . . for
> He is the mid-Point of all thing.
>
> JULIAN OF NORWICH [40]

SOMEONE HAS SUGGESTED that the symbol for modern man is fission—a breaking up of relationships, an eruption into disunity. It is obvious that there is some truth in the statement. And if this is so, then the remedy which our time needs is the one Christ offers, for he is the center of unity for man. He is (in T. S. Eliot's phrase) the "still point of the turning world." He is God, and here is Dante's description of his vision of the Godhead: "I saw a Point which radiated light [and] around the Point a circle of light whirled . . . and this was circumscribed [by other circles]. On that Point, the heavens and all of Nature depend" (*Paradiso* 28:16 ff.).

Before we begin, however, to talk of Christ's central position, it may be well to look back over the way we have come, for this chapter is the center of the book, the mid-point where one stops to look back and to look forward.

1. *The view from the center: review and preview*

Our progress thus far has been something like climbing a mountain. We have now reached a level place and can stop to see how far we have come. This will give us courage to go on. It may even be that we will feel exhilaration at our accomplishment—a delight like that which Eunice Tietjens describes in her poem, "The Most-Sacred Mountain": [41]

> Space, and the twelve clean winds of heaven,
> And this sharp exultation, like a cry, after the
>   slow six thousand feet of climbing! . . .
>
> Below my feet the foot-hills nestle, brown with
>   flecks of green; and lower down . . . the
>   floor of earth stretches away to blue infinity.
>
> Beside me in this airy space the temple roofs cut
>   their slow curves against the sky,
> And one black bird circles above the void.
> Space, and the twelve clean winds are here;
> And with them broods eternity—a swift white peace,
>   a presence manifest. . . .

Perhaps we, too, feel as if we have done a "slow six thousand feet of climbing," for a great many ideas have been explored in the first chapters.

But the next ascent should be easier. We may even be able to begin our last lap with an exultation so sharp it is "like a cry." For, as was said long ago in the introduction, it is a joy to gain insight into the wonders of God's ways. And a particular delight is ours when we admire the unity he effects by his use of earthly things for superearthly purposes. Once these insights are ours we feel like saying with the speaker in the same poem:

> [I must] go down from this airy space, this swift
> white peace, this stinging exultation;
> And time will close about me, and my soul stir
> to the rhythm of the daily round.
> Yet, having known, life will not press so close,
> and always I shall feel time ravel thin
> about me;
> For once I stood in the white windy presence of
> eternity.

With the thought of the value to us of knowing these things, let us next turn to our review of the things we have seen.

In our over-view of the way we have come, we might take the word *recurrent* as a key for our understanding. We have thought of the liturgy as designed in the recurrent movement of circles—a patterned repetition like that of a wheel, or the curves set in motion by a stone dropped in water, or the wheeling of the planets.

We have also seen that these circles are invested with significance because of the recurrent theme of transfiguration. And we realize that recurring symbols, particularly those related to the four elements of earth, air, fire, and water, can be found enriching the liturgy with variety, and channeling God's transfiguring action to man. Recurrence is therefore a feature of design, theme, and symbols.

The circular design, we have felt, was particularly appropriate for use in describing the liturgy because it symbolizes two of man's basic needs. First it stands for the stability characteristic of the unmoving center of the ring and for the security which is a feature of its persistent return. Second, change and progress are also naturally symbolized by the rim of the circle on which the wheel travels, and which, even when it is stationary, tempts our eyes and mind to move around its circumference. These qualities of stability and progress, of stillness and movement, are clearly exemplified, as we shall see in the four large divisions of the liturgy.

Furthermore, we have realized that the circles of nature, as seen in man's life and the day and the year, may become a monotonous recurrence, or worse yet, a narrowing spiral closing in on itself—diminishing until it ends in death. But in the liturgy this recurrence is more than repetition, and it is not a narrowing, but an expanding spiral. Or perhaps we might better describe its revolving circles as continually widening, taking in more of God and of nature with each cycle, until at last all the circles burst with the final coming of Christ, and there remain only uncircumscribed, unlimited joy and peace.

In our preparation for a closer contemplation of the Mass and the other circles, we have also seen that the theme of transfiguration brings unity and meaning to the design. It functions as themes do in art: framing Christian life between the significance of two anointings, and appearing according to a pattern of rhythm which presents the theme at first partially and with variations. These variations then cumulate until the climax of man's life is reached with the vision of God; and the climax of creation comes with the second and triumphant appearance of Christ at the end of the world.

This theme has, moreover, one natural and two supernatural effects. We have named these the epiphanal or revelational, sacrificial or gift-giving, and sacramental or gift-receiving effects of transfiguration.

Finally, in our discussion of symbols and symbolism we have found that man needs to reawaken his awareness of nature, and that the natural symbolism of the liturgy can help him do this. Our view of symbols has found them marked by three characteristics: 1) they exist on the material level, where we admire and value them. 2) At the same time they signify a spiritual or intellectual meaning beyond themselves. 3) This meaning is usually rich and complex rather than simple. Lastly, the most important and frequently recurring symbols are those based on the four elements: earth, air, fire, and water.

It will be the business of the next four chapters to show these concepts as actually operating in the Mass, the sacraments, the day, and the year.

Because these principles are recurrent, because they function in repetitive and rhythmical patterns, a certain unity is apparent in the whole majestic structure. This is the first artistic principle. Variety, the second, is also apparent in many ways. One way, for example, in which it operates, is through the secondary patterns of action which occur within the large circular movement. These will be discussed at some length later.

Such patterns within patterns might be compared to the elliptical whirling of the earth on its axis, which takes place simultaneously with its steady course around the sun. Or again we might say the pattern is like the movement of the moon around the earth while earth goes around the sun.

An example of this double pattern will be studied in some detail in chapter five where we consider the action of the Mass. Here we will see that the Mass not only moves in circular return of worship, and constant re-presentation of Christ's mysteries, but also that each Mass is clearly structured in a system of sacrificial actions which express its whole purpose. This second structured movement is not circular in form.

For a simpler example of recurrence which yet avoids monotony, take the ever present symbol of light as it glows and gleams and flames in the yearly cycle. On the first Sunday of Advent the light begins to appear, and we hear in the epistle: "The night is far on its course; day draws near" (Rom. 13:12). This is true because Christ, the dawn of salvation will come soon in the feast of Christmas.

Then at Easter, holding high the Paschal candle, which is a symbol of the risen Christ, the Church, through the voice of her priest, sings: "*Lumen Christi*—the light of Christ."

And all, seeing the light clearly before them, leading them to the altar of God, sing *"Deo gratias*—thanks be to God."

Thirdly, at Pentecost, the light is again transformed, for now the Church speaks to us of the fiery tongues which the Holy Spirit used to signify his coming. The light in this case no longer rests on the body of a candle, but it is wholly heavenly. It no longer reaches up to God out of a material body, as we have seen the candle as symbol of Christ, God and man, doing, but instead the flame comes down from heaven and rests on each Christian present in the supper room. Now these Christians themselves become candles, as it were. They are new Christs, ready to bear the flame of the Spirit out to light the world.

From the dawn coming up out of night, to the candle of the glorified Christ plain for our seeing, to the Pentecostal tongues of fire transfiguring Christians into new Christ-candles, the progression can be followed. Yet all these different images rest on the one symbol of light.

Recurrence and variation, unity and variety, these mark the design, theme, and symbols of the liturgy. But we are now going to be especially interested in one aspect of unity, namely, Christ as the center, the point on which everything depends, and towards which everything tends. This unity rests firmly on the centrality of Christ, as this chapter will point out. Through his power the four circles of Mass, sacraments, office, liturgical seasons, move. Everything in them is transfigured and given meaning by his presence and his action, and it is into his likeness that men are transfigured by their instrumentality.

2. *Christ the center of the design*

According to the design, then, Christ is the point at the center. And circumscribing him we find the four circles of the Mass, the sacramental system, the consecration of the day, and the feasts and fasts of the year.

The idea of God as a point is a very old one. The mystics frequently speak of finding him in the deepest point of their being. Julian of Norwich, for example, says, "I saw God in a Point . . . by which sight I saw that He is in all things. [I saw] the working of our Lord God in the creature: for He is the mid-Point of all thing." Euclid, too, is reported as calling both the point and the circle immeasurable. And it is because of this notion that both are frequently used as symbols for God.

Christ the still point, however, is at the same time a radiating point and a point of magnetic attraction—a kind of center of gravity. His power, in other words, is both centripetal and centrifugal. St. Paul clearly describes both movements.

He says, "It was [God's] loving design, centered in Christ, to give history its fulfillment by *resuming* everything in him, all that is in heaven, all that is on earth, *summed up* in him" (Eph. 1:10-11). This expresses particularly the centripetal force of Christ. It says in a different manner what he himself once said: "If only I am lifted up from the earth, I will attract all men to myself" (John 12:31). This is a magnetic power which holds everything in place—as the planets are held in place by the centripetal force of their suns.

The other effect is a centrifugal, or radiating force. St. Paul expresses the idea this way: "All things find in him their origin, their *impulse,* the center of their being" (Rom. 11:36). We might think of this again in terms of the sun, but now we are aware that the sun not only holds the planets in their orbits, but that it also radiates warmth and light; thus in a certain way it projects itself into these other things, and by its power it transforms these natural worlds.

The illustrations for chapters seven and eight on the sacraments and office respectively, illustrate these centrifugal and centripetal powers of Christ in the liturgy. Notice how in the first of these pictures, the rays of the sacraments radiate out from him to warm the world into holiness, while in the second they are focused inward, drawing the daily praise of man toward Christ.

Under such figures we see Christ, by a magnetizing movement, "resuming everything in him [self], all that is in heaven, all that is on earth, summed up in him" (Eph. 1:10); we see also that by a radiating movement, he permeates all things with his significance and power.

Through this radiating movement, God's power reaches out from Christ to invade man's innermost being (Eph. 3:16), and to "fill creation with his presence" (Eph. 4:10). From him, as from the sun, the light of wisdom and the warmth of love radiate, and coming into contact with all created things, they fill them with vivifying rays. Then again, in a return movement which is a completion of the circle, Christ once more draws all things to himself, and his power operates to transfigure men into his own image.

3. *Centripetal effect*

Christ is, therefore, the center where time and eternity, space and transpatial reality, the things of men and the things of God, come together. Like the point at the center of a whirlpool, he draws all towards the center.

He is the center because the fullness of the Godhead is in him. He is a person of the one God, and where he, the Word, is, there is the Father sending him forth, and the Spirit flaming out from their mutual love. Hence the whole Godhead is here, in Christ, at the center of things.

Christ, our Lord, moreover, is not only God, he is also man. Because he has assumed our nature, and even more because he has, by grace, given us a share in his divine nature, therefore our humanity is at the center with Christ. In such wonderful ways does God manifest "the splendour of that grace by which he has taken us into his favour in the person of his beloved Son" (Eph. 1:6).

Finally, it is not only divinity and humanity which are unified in Christ, but even the lower levels of creation have some share in this glory. This comes about because Christ, in his human nature, had a material body—a body constituted of chemical elements having vegetative and animal powers. Thus animate and inanimate worlds are drawn into unity in Christ.

To illustrate some of these centripetal powers, let us consider the prayer said at the mingling of water and wine during the offertory of the Mass. The priest prays:

> O God, by whom the dignity of human nature was wondrously established and yet more wondrously restored, grant that through the sacramental rite of this water and wine we may have fellowship in the Godhead of him who didst share our manhood, Jesus Christ, thy Son, our Lord, who is God, living and reigning with thee in the unity of the Holy Spirit . . .

In this prayer the priest (and we with him) praises God because of the wonders which took place in his first creation of man. We say that it was by his power that "the dignity of human nature was [first] wondrously established." This is one mystery.

Then we go on to tell of a yet more wonderful event—the restoring of man to God's friendship, to his sharing in supernatural life, when through man's own fault he had lost his privileges. This redemption was accomplished by Christ at the time of his death and resurrection.

Here, then, is the first unifying, centripetal note in the prayer. We find, when we penetrate the surface of the words, that here Christ draws together, he unifies once more, the two who have been separated—God and man. This redemption is, therefore, one aspect of Christ's unifying action. And it is commemorated in this prayer where we speak of the wonderful way God has chosen to restore human nature to its privileges—so that while it was once "wondrously established," it now is "yet more wondrously restored."

The prayer goes on to present a petition for still further unity: "grant that through the sacramental rite of this water and wine we may have fellowship in the Godhead of [Christ]." Here we ask that we may be united with Christ, and through him with the whole Godhead. We pray that we may be so closely united with him that we may share his Godhead, his divine life itself. We ask that this may come about as a sacramental effect of the mingling of the water with the wine. Thus we are saying by our symbolic actions as well as by our words that we wish this to be a total and indissoluble union—a union like that of the few drops of water received into the wine and wholly penetrated by its properties.

Next we speak with greater boldness, more confident expectation. We act almost as if this "trading" of Christ's Godhead to us in exchange for our manhood were a fair bargain. This is what the Christmas liturgy calls the *admirabile commercium*—the wonderful exchange. And emphasizing this idea of an exchange we say: "Grant us to have fellowship in the Godhead of him who didst share our manhood." In other words, we imply, audaciously but in all reverence, that since we have given our manhood to Christ, it is not beyond possibility that he will give us a share of his Godhead in return.

The prayer then ends as it began, with praise. He is "Jesus Christ thy Son who is God" and he "lives and reigns" with God. This structuring of the prayer is most interesting, for such a sandwiching of petition between two sections of praise is characteristic of the Church's prayers of petition. One needs only to glance at collects, secrets, and post-communions of the Mass to see the prevalence of the design.

Over and over again we find structures like this of the offertory petition. To make the scaffolding clearer, let us paraphrase the meaning. We say: 1) O God, who hast done this deed (whatever specific thing it may be) in such an admirable way, we glorify you. 2) Now please grant us this certain favor. 3) You ought to grant it because we ask it of you in the name of your Son who lives with you and rules heaven and earth. Such is the threefold structure of this prayer, and of nearly every petitionary prayer in the liturgy. And the meaning of this prayer is a centripetal one. In it we ask that all things may be unified in and through Christ.

4. *Centrifugal effect*

The second or radiating function of Christ the center, can be seen in the prayer which occurs at the end of the sacrifice proper. Here is the prayer:

> It is ever through him that all these good gifts created by thee, Lord, are by thee sanctified, endowed with life, blessed, and bestowed upon us. Through him, and with him, and in him, thou, God, almighty Father, in the unity of the Holy Spirit, hast all honour and glory.

Here we discover that Christ, the Word of God, radiates power: 1) at creation ("Through him . . . all good gifts created . . . are . . . endowed with life"); 2) in sanctifying and bestowing all good gifts ("blessed, and bestowed upon us"); 3) in giving all praise to God ("Through him . . . thou . . . hast all honour and glory").

In the prayer we first recollect that all things were created through the word of God who is here present on the altar. As St. John in the prologue to his gospel says, "Without him was made nothing that was made." In other words, God was not content to keep his joy and love within the Trinity of persons, but through his Son and with his Spirit, the Father, as it were, stirred his changelessness and created our ever changing world. This is one aspect of the power which radiates from the second person, the Word, who is Christ our Lord.

Then we go on, in the prayer, to rejoice in the fact that all good gifts, all created things, are sanctified, endowed with life, blessed, and bestowed upon us through Christ. Through his centrifugal power, all the good things we receive are made holy and invested with life. And through him they are given to us.

This prayer ends with the beautiful doxology which closes the canon, the unchanging sacrificial part of the Mass. The priest says, "Through him, and with him, and in him, thou, God, almighty Father, in the unity of the Holy Spirit, hast all honour and glory." When he has said this, he raises his voice in the words which are commonly used as a closing for prayer: *"per omnia saecula saeculorum—*world without end." After these words we signify our agreement by saying *Amen.* By this we show our sharing in the gift-giving which has just taken place.

The action we have consented to is the upward and outward movement from us with Christ towards the Father. By this action in the Mass, Christ, God's own Son, offers himself, through the hands of the priest, and with our active support, as our gift to the Father for his and the Holy Spirit's glory.

Christ, then, is the center—a center which draws us towards itself, that being drawn in to him we may be transfigured into his likeness. And he is also the radiating center, sending out his power to fill the world with supernatural light and warmth, as the natural sun fills the world with life-giving warmth and light.

In the next chapter we shall discuss the sacrifice of the Mass, the first circle circumscribing the center. We shall first talk of its inner structure of action, the design which signifies and effects the sacrifice, and secondly, of the functioning of the four elements in its various parts.

SECOND PART

CHAPTER SIX

Of the Mass: First Circle

> Thus says the Lord, Heaven is my throne, earth the footstool under my feet. . . . Nothing you see . . . but I fashioned it . . . my hand gave it being. From whom then shall I accept an offering?
>
> *Isaias,* 66:1-2

THE FIRST and inmost circle around Christ the center is that of the Mass. It possesses the circle's renewal and stability —its dynamism and its changelessness. In its essence, the Mass is changeless, for it is the one sacrifice of the same Christ who died on Calvary and rose again to walk the roads of Galilee— that Christ who, since the ascension, is at the right hand of the Father, always living to remind the Father of us.

But this changeless sacrifice is always new, because with each Mass it enters into a particular place at a special moment of time. In this way each generation and each man can make contact with Christ. Every Christian can lift him up as his own gift to the Father, and every man who so wishes can receive Christ back again as the Father's best gift to us.

In these ways the essence of the Mass and its manifestation to men is marked with unity and variety, changelessness and dynamism. And not only the inner reality of the Mass is always old and always new—marked with unity and variety—

but also the Mass is changeless and changing in its effects and in its structure.

Let us think first about the effects of the Mass. They are always the same because every Christian offers the same Christ, and receives his graces. But they differ because every man comes to Mass with a different preparation and capacity. These differences appear in the effect of the Mass on each individual and its effects on the whole living organism of the mystical body of Christ.

In the case of the latter, the Mass can, in a certain way, be said to have a greater effect each time it is celebrated. Why? Because with each Mass the members of Christ's body are here and now strengthened, united more firmly to Christ and each other, deepened in capacity for love and grace.

With each Mass, therefore, all Christians move toward the "completion of him who everywhere and in all things is complete" (Eph. 1:23). In this sense we can say that the effects of today's Mass are always greater than those of yesterday's. This is true because the mystical body of Christ is today, in St. Paul's words, more complete. And being more complete, it is possessed of a greater receptivity to grace and a greater power for good.

When we think of the differences in the effect of the Mass on each man, an example may help. We might compare the sameness and difference with the daily rising of the sun. It is always the same sun that rises, just as it is always the same Christ in the Mass. But the effects of the dawn are modified by the conditions of earth and air. One morning the sun comes up in a blaze, another day the mist diffuses its brightness; some dawns are slow, others swift. As the earth brings something to the sun and together they make the dawn, so man brings something to the Mass.

He brings his own effort at preparation, his alertness, his active participation. Each one brings all his yesterdays—the experiences, the talents, the generosity which have made him what he is. Most important of all, he brings his own "joyful surrender," which he unites with the surrender of Christ to his Father. This means that every person has a different degree of acceptance toward all that the Mass can do in the transfiguring of his daily life in its practical details. Each man, therefore, along with Christ, brings about the particular effects of grace in him, his own special dawn. This is one kind of variety.

Finally there is unity with variety in the very architecture, the structure of the Mass. There are in it two patterns of movement. One of these patterns follows the circling of the year. It can be traced in the *proper* of the Mass which changes every day. The other movement is that based on the *ordinary* —the unchanging part of the Mass. This serves to structure the sacrificial prayer and action. We might say that the movement of the proper is like the circling of the earth around the sun. This will be considered in the last chapter of this book. The other movement, that of the ordinary, might (in one way) be compared to the turning of the earth on its axis, which goes on at the same time that the world makes the larger circle.

But from another point of view, this secondary design is not so much a circle as it is an up and down movement—a rising and returning pattern which we might compare with the rising of moisture from the earth into the air, its transformation by condensation, and its return to the earth as rain. It is this last pattern which will be discussed in the first half of the present chapter.

As we have seen, the Mass presents a rich pattern of unity and variety: in its inner reality, in its effects, and in its double structure. It signifies realities too great for us to grasp without the help of symbolic materials and actions, and so our concern here will be with the actions and the symbols of the sacrifice. The purpose of the Mass is to offer an adequate worship to God, and man in offering this worship undergoes a transformation—a transfiguration through the ineffable working of God's power. Now let us look a little more closely at the structure of the Mass ordinary.

1. *The structure of the Mass*

> "Only by the form, the pattern,
> Can words or music reach
> The stillness . . ."
>
> T. S. ELIOT

The Mass takes an upward, sacrificial direction towards God, and a downward, sacramental movement from God to man. In the simplest possible terms we might describe this up and down movement by saying that there are five main actions in each Mass, arranged in a symmetrical pattern. Two of these, the offertory and communion, are simple straightforward movements, the other three are more complex. Here is a sketch of the design:

1. We speak to God and God speaks to us in the Fore-Mass.
2. We give a gift to God (bread, wine, ourselves) in the offertory.
3. God accepts and transforms this gift, and then we offer the transformed gift, (which is Christ) to the Father in the canon.
4. God shares the gift (of Christ) with us in the communion.
5. We speak to God and God speaks to us at the end.

We might think of this pattern as a diagram like the letter *M* with two small pyramids, or inverted letter *V*'s on each side. Look at the figure on this page. If we begin at the point farthest left and follow the lines we will catch some of the rhythm of the Mass. It will help even to trace out the lines with a finger. Do it this way: 1) We speak to God—the line goes up; God speaks to us—down. 2) We offer our human and earthly gifts—the lines goes up. 3) God bends down to accept them—slant line down; Christ acting through his priest transubstantiates, changing the substance of bread and wine into his own Body and Blood—mid-point of the M; then we lift Christ up as our perfect gift to the Father—slant line up. 4) God gives his gift of Christ to us—the long line goes down. 5) We speak to God—up; God speaks to us—down. In the design which illustrates this chapter, the small circles around the M present symbols for each of these five parts of the Mass.

Because of this symmetry of motion the Mass has been called a sacred ceremonial dance. We know how naturally man tends to express his feelings in the dance. A child pretending to be a bird or a tree may dance with perfect spontaneity; an Indian war dance expresses another emotion. Then again, there are the picturesque and reverent dances certain tribes perform as a petition for rain. And long ago, David laid aside his royal dignity—or better, he invested himself with greater dignity—and danced in worship before the Ark of the Covenant.

Then again, because of the interchange of speech and action, the Holy Sacrifice has been described as a great drama. It is this. But of course, it is also more than drama—more than play acting. It is more, because the act that is here dramatized comes true in the doing. We re-enact the Last Supper and Calvary and they are actualized here and now.

Finally because of the wealth of its meaning and its symbolic images (which we shall discuss in the second half of this chapter), it might be called a ritual poem. In this connection, it is well to remark here that a single image does not usually make a poem. And even more certainly a single image can seldom be accepted as carrying symbolic meaning.

Symbols, rather, gather up meanings by a process of accretion. And this is particularly true in the liturgy. One mention of water or fire does not give the element any depth of meaning. But when water is spoken of with almost rhythmic regularity, sometimes in quiet everyday situations, again in the context of miraculous happenings, as occurs in scripture, then we begin to feel that there is more to its significance than at first appears.

Whether we look at the Mass, then, as a reverent dance, as a drama which comes true in the doing, or as a richly significant poem, it possesses the qualities necessary to make it an admirable work of art. Yet on the other hand, the Mass was not planned as a work of art. It was rather shaped in such a way as to make it the supreme act of worship. As Guardini says, it was "not built up . . . for the pleasure of forming beautiful symbols, choice language, and . . . stately gestures, but for the sake of our desperate spiritual need . . . to give expression to . . . the assimilation of the life of the creature to the life of God in Christ." [42]

If the Mass were totally without artistic value it would still be the greatest speech and the greatest action man can share in. The speech is conversation with God, which we call prayer. The action is an interchange of gifts: man's giftgiving to God which is sacrifice; God's giving to man, which is sacrament.

Now suppose that someone, in conversation with another person, were to answer at intervals: Yes; yes; yes; yes; thanks be to God—*Yes,* four times, and then a strong expression of gratitude. Suppose again that this complete agreement was spoken, not by one alone, but by a great crowd of people who gave their consent out of deep conviction. Everyone would admit that something momentous was happening.

Now this is just what happens every day at Mass, for as we have begun to see, the Mass falls into five sections. Moreover, after each of these sections we say *Amen—Yes,* until we reach the last, when we say *Deo gratias*—Thanks be to God.

Amen is a word of consent, of affirmation. Someone has said that God's favorite word is *yes,* and at Mass we say this favorite word of God's again and again, especially at the end of each main division. Sometimes we say it silently, at other times we sing or say it aloud. This depends on the particular circumstances in which we are when we participate in the great action. Then at the close of the whole wonderful drama, we say *Deo gratias*—Thanks be to God.

The action of the Mass is symmetrical, rhythmic, but more than this, it is meaningful, and it is powerful in its effects. Let us look more closely now at the way it is structured, for the structure expresses the meaning, and channels the power.

First of all, the three sections of action are framed—they are enclosed and wrought into unity—between two sections of speech, of dialogue. Furthermore, each of the five sections not only closes, as we have said, with a word of affirmation, but each also opens with a call to attention. This call may appear in the shape of a resolution to proceed, a greeting for a journey, or a prayer indicating readiness for further progress. Each of the five sections, therefore is strengthened in its inner unity because of this framing between a greeting and an affirmation.

The first and last sections, therefore, consist of speech, as we have said. The middle ones constitute the action of the sacrifice. Within the framework of the drama, prayer and sacrifice and sacrament take place. Here is a chart showing these various facets of the five divisions:

We are now ready to trace the design in more detail and in orderly fashion just as it happens during Mass.

(i) *Fore-Mass*

First, during the Fore-Mass, or Mass of Catechumens, we speak to God. In Psalm 42, we say "I will go up to the altar

The Mass: Its Five Divisions

Content	Section	Opening	Happening	Ending (assent)
Speech	Fore-Mass	"I will go up to the altar . . ."	We speak to God in Ps. 42, Confiteor, Introit, Kyrie, Gloria, Collects, Credo. God speaks to us in Epistle or Lesson, Gospel, Sermon.	*Amen* after Credo. If no creed, then "Praise be to thee, O Christ," after Gospel
Action (sacrifice)	Offertory	"The Lord be with you"	We offer mortal gifts: bread, wine, ourselves.	*Amen* after Secret prayers
Action (consecration & sacrifice)	Canon	"The Lord be with you"	God accepts our mortal offerings. The gifts are transubstantiated. We then offer Christ.	*Amen* after doxology: "Through him, and with him. . ."
Action (sacrament)	Communion	Prayer before *Pater Noster*	God gives Christ to us.	*Amen* after Post-communion
Speech	Close of Mass	"The Lord be with you"	We speak to God in summary prayer. God speaks to us in Last Gospel.	*Deo gratias* after last Gospel

of God." We begin, therefore, with a resolution. Then we sing to him in the Introit, which changes daily, and sets the special theme of each Mass. In the Confiteor, we admit that we are sinners. As a result of our realization of unworthiness, we ask for God's mercy in the Kyrie. Then we sing the Gloria and rejoice in God's greatness. Finally, in the Collects, we present specific petitions which are different each day.

Secondly, God speaks to us in the Epistle and Gospel, and in the sermon if there is one. After hearing his words, we signify our faith and our assent to his will in one of two ways. Either we say the Credo, a kind of pledge of allegiance to God, which ends with the affirmation word, Amen. Or if there is no creed, we speak our affirmation at the end of the Gospel by saying, "Praise be to thee, O Christ." This is the end of the first section of the Mass, the pyramid on the left of the *M* in the illustration at the beginning of this chapter.

(ii) *Offertory*

The action begins in the second part of the Mass with the offertory. This section is framed between the greeting, *Dominus vobiscum*, and the consent of our *Amen*. During the offertory we lift up our gifts of bread, wine, and ourselves to God. These are not very expensive gifts, but they represent all we have. Later in the Mass, God will make them more valuable.

In this section, nearly every prayer mentions offering, sacrifice, or victim. Thus the gift-giving meaning is kept before our minds. Our gifts, as we have said, are bread and wine and our human selves. The bread is literally bread, and the wine is truly wine. These literal realities are not lost later on when we begin to think of symbolic meanings for them.

Toward the end of the offertory, the priest invites us to join our intentions yet more closely to the sacrifice. He says aloud, "*Orate, fratres,*" that is, "Pray, brethren," and immediately we pray that the Lord may receive our sacrifice at the priest's hands "to the praise and glory of [God's] name, for our good, and that of the whole world."

This "Pray, brethren," is a signal which tells us that it is almost time for our final ratifying of the offertory. Immediately after the signal, the priest begins to sum up the intentions of the people in the prayers called Secrets. The name indicates that the prayers are said silently. But it is also related to the word *secretion,* which means a gathering together. Here, then, as in the Mass Collect, all our varied intentions are gathered up and presented with our oblation.

At the end of the Secret prayers, the priest says aloud a phrase which serves as the closing formula for many prayers: *"Per omnia saecula saeculorum*—for ever and ever." The meaning is: "May God reign for ever and ever; may he be praised for ever and ever." Here the formula indicates to us that the offertory is finished. All of us signify our assent to the completed offertory by saying *Amen.* And we are ready for the next part.

(iii) *Canon*

The third part of the Mass, called the canon, is framed exactly as the offertory was. It also opens with the greeting, *"Dominus vobiscum*—the Lord be with you," which is a kind of invitation to travel along in company with Christ. To this we answer, *"Et cum spiritu tuo*—and with you." The canon, moreover, closes as the offertory does, with an *Amen.*

In the action of this section, the Father accepts our human and earthly gifts. Then by the working of his almighty power, and through the instrumentality of his priest, who acts in Christ's name, the transubstantiation is effected. By this change, what was before simply bread and wine becomes the body and blood, soul and divinity of our Lord Jesus Christ. After this, our gift is a present completely worthy of God— it is his own divine Son in whom he is well pleased.

Immediately after the consecration, we, through the priest's hands, lift up our transfigured gift as a perfect sacrifice to God. The prayer which follows the consecration emphasizes this note of sacrifice:

> And now, Lord, we thy servants, and with us all thy holy people, calling to mind the blessed Passion of this same Christ, thy Son, our Lord, likewise his resurrection from the grave, and glorious ascension into heaven, *offer to thy sovereign majesty, out of the gifts thou hast bestowed upon us, a sacrifice* that is pure, holy and unblemished, the sacred Bread of everlasting life, and the Cup of eternal salvation (Italics added).

In this place we, as it were, gather together and offer to God all of the mysteries of Christ: his "passion, resurrection, and glorious ascension." Here, in Bouyer's words, we witness the fact that "in Christ the fullness of God giving Himself to man meets with the fullness of man offering himself to God." [43]

This most important section of the Mass continues with some prayers which refer repeatedly to the sacrificial action being performed here. Then finally it ends with the *Amen* after the wonderful closing prayer of praise: "It is ever through him that all these good gifts [all of earth and all of heaven, in Christ] are created, sanctified, endowed with life, and bestowed upon us . . ." At the end of this prayer, said by the priest and concurred in by us, he pronounces aloud the familiar formula: "For ever and ever." Then all the people, at least in their hearts, answer *Amen*. This is the greatest Amen in the whole Mass, the concluding word of the whole sacrificial action.

By this last prayer we have reminded ourselves that all good gifts come to us from God ("all these good gifts created by thee . . . are . . . bestowed upon us"). And when we offer him our sacrifices we are only giving back the things which he first gave us. This reminds us of our creatureliness, and so places us in an attitude of adoration and receptivity suitable for the next section of the Mass. In it, God will give us the gift of his Son.

(iv) *Communion*

As God was pleased with the earlier, less valuable, gifts of bread and wine and ourselves, and showed his pleasure by transforming the gifts into something greater, so he is even more pleased by the present we now offer. This is our gift to him of his own divine Son. And here again he shows his pleased acceptance, but this time in a different way. This time he shares his present with us. He gives us his own Son in Holy Communion.

This section of the Mass, the communion, begins with the short preparatory prayer before the *Our Father.* Here it is: "Urged by our Saviour's bidding, and schooled by his divine ordinance, we make bold to say: 'Our Father . . .' " The prayer implies that the Mass we have been offering has made us more ready than we were before to call God our Father, and to come to his banquet table in Holy Communion. We might take the words as saying: Since Christ has invited us (by his *bidding*), and since he has taught us how (schooled us) to do it, therefore we are ready to say *"Pater Noster*—Our Father." [44]

Perhaps the meaning will become even clearer if we think about the two verbals in the prayer as it is said in Latin. Here we see: *moniti* and *formati* which mean *taught* and *formed.* Using these words as keys to the significance of the prayer, it is possible to find here a summary of the Mass we have thus far offered, and also of its effects on us.

According to this interpretation, we have been *taught* by the things which God has said to us in the Fore-Mass. We have learned from the Church, our teacher. And we have been *formed,* given another "shape," changed and transfigured, by the sacrificial part of the Mass, the offertory and the canon. These have deepened in us the likeness to Christ, who lived only for his Father's glory, just as we, too, have been saying by our sacrifice, that we wish to live for God. We know that our Lord states clearly this central purpose of his life: "The world must be convinced," he says, "that I love the Father, and act only as the Father has commanded me to act" (John 14:31). This is the very thing our Mass says for us.

St. Paul, also, tells us that when Christ came into the world he said: "See, my God, I am coming to do thy will" (Heb. 10:9). The very food which keeps him alive, our Lord says, is his Father's will: "My meat is to do the will of him who sent me" (John 4:34). Now it is especially in the Mass that Christ invests us with this disposition of his—this total turning of his whole life towards his Father. And by this total and Christlike dedication to God, we are made fruitful Christians.

It is particularly by our offering made at Mass that we give ourselves wholly to God. Then our "meat" too, becomes the doing of his will. We find, then, that what Dante says is true: "In his will is our peace" (Paradiso 3:85).

Moreover, in our sacrificial action we are primarily interested in furthering God's glory, without being too much concerned with ourselves. By such a God-ward attitude, we grow to resemble Christ more closely. We are transfigured. Therefore, when the Father looks at us, as we are now, after offering Mass, he sees in us an image—and more than this, a living member—of his beloved Son in whom he is well pleased.

Because we are now taught and formed in all these ways, we are ready to call God our Father. And we are ready, moreover, to come to the table and share a sacramental meal with our Father.

After this short but important introductory prayer, the *Pater Noster* is said. This, and the prayers which follow it are preparations for, and thanksgivings after Holy Communion. Fittingly enough, all through this part of the Mass we find constant references to food, and home, and hospitality. This symbolism of sharing a meal continues until after the short prayers called the postcommunions. These postcommunions change with the different feasts, and frequently they mention the fact that this food of the Eucharist is intended to nourish and strengthen us, just as the ordinary food we eat strengthens and nourishes our bodies. The postcommunion for the third Sunday after Easter, for example, clearly expresses this thought: "May the sacrament we have taken, Lord, fill us with spiritual food and comfort us with bodily support."

At the end of the postcommunion prayers, the priest gives us the now familiar closing signal, the expected formula of "world without end." This is our cue in the drama. It is our time once more to indicate our consent to all that God has been doing in us and for us during the Mass. We therefore answer *Amen,* and with this significant word the communion section closes.

(v) *End of Mass*

Now comes the greeting once more: "The Lord be with you," and along with it comes a reminder that in a few moments we will set out from this holy place. We will go back to our daily life. The priest says, for this purpose: *"Ite, missa est*—Go, this is the dismissal." The phrase may be taken as a command to carry the fruits of our Mass out into our homes, our work, our recreation. After this injunction we hold a short conversation, a kind of farewell dialogue, which balances the exchange of speech between God and ourselves at the beginning of the Mass. In this later dialogue, we ask that the most holy Trinity may be pleased with the sacrifice we have been offering.

In response to this, the priest, in the name of the whole Trinity, gives us a blessing. And finally, we listen to the last gospel—God's last word to us in this Mass. It is the prologue to St. John's gospel, which reminds us once again that

Christ is truly the Father's beloved Son in whom he is well pleased. This is, in a way, an answer to our prayer that the sacrifice might be acceptable. For if the Christ we have offered is truly God's own divine Son, then the implication is that God cannot help but be pleased with the gift.

St. John, in this gospel, calls Christ the life and the light: "In him there was life, and that life was the light of men. And the light shines in darkness . . . he was the true Light." In this ending, with its references to Christ as the light that shines in darkness, we can discover symbols for the beginning of our world.

We have mentioned earlier the first words of Genesis: "God at the beginning of time, created heaven and earth. Earth was still an empty waste, and darkness hung over the deep; but already over its waters, brooded the spirit of God. Then God said, Let there be light; and the light began. God saw the light and found it good" (Gen. 1:1-4).

Now in this ending of the Mass, John who wrote the last of the four gospels, picks up these Genesis images and uses them to refer to the eternity of the Word with the Father, and to the beginnings of creation. John says: "At the beginning of time the Word already was; and God had the Word abiding with him, and the Word was God. It was through him that all things came into being, and without him came nothing that has come to be. In him there was life, and that life was the light of men. And the light shines in darkness. . . . He was the true Light. He through whom the world was made . . ."

In this passage, John catches the mysterious tone of Genesis. He carries us in a contemplative circling motion back to the beginnings of all things. And just as the first thing God made was light, so John thinks of light and tells us that in a certain sense the light which *was* already when creation began is the Light of God's eternal Word, his Wisdom. Through him the created light came to be.

With this reminder of new beginnings, we come to the end of Mass. And we think of the offertory prayer quoted much earlier, where man's two beginnings of creation and of redemption are listed in praise: "O God, by whom the dignity of human nature was wondrously established [at creation] and yet more wondrously restored [at redemption]"—and then we realize that this new creation, this fresh redemption is here actualized in the Mass.

Now, after Mass, we are ready to make a new beginning of another kind. We are ready to go out refreshed and strengthened into the start of a new day. In our chapter, too, we are finished with our survey of the Mass structure, and are ready to go back to the beginning—the start of the Mass. We will, therefore, in this second half of the chapter, think first about the symbolism of the Mass in general, and afterwards about the symbols of each part in particular.

2. *The four elements as symbols in the Mass*

> Music of elements, that a miracle makes!
> Earth, air, water, fire, singing into
> the white Act.
>
> DYLAN THOMAS [45]

In God's last word to us in the Mass, we have just seen that the Word of God was with the Father when he created heaven and earth—when he made water and air, fire and the land. We might put into the mouth of this divine Word the saying from the Book of Wisdom:

> I was there when he built the heavens, when he fenced in the waters with a vault inviolable, when he fixed the sky overhead . . . when he poised the foundations of the world. (Proverbs, 8:27-29)

When all the elements were made, the Word of God was at the Father's side, his "delight increasing with each day, as

[he] made play in this world of dust" (Prov. 8:30-31). From the very beginning, as this shows, the Word was delighted with creation.

It is only natural, then, that the Mass which brings this Word in his humanity in a special way into creation—into our time and space—should be filled with symbols signifying all the creatures in the round world, and especially the elements of earth, air, fire, and water. There are in it the things of earth: symbols related to earth's surface and its extension in space; namely, mountains, shelters, journeys. And we find also, symbols related to earth's fruitfulness: the lamb, bread, wine. Here, too, are symbols of air—smoke and fragrance and the breath of man; and symbols of that fire which burns and enlightens. Finally there are, in the Mass, symbols from water with its cleansing and fructifying qualities.

In discussing the function of these symbols, we shall first present an over-view of the five sections, next we shall discuss the Exodus symbol of the journey, which is central to the meaning of the Mass. Only after this, shall we take the symbols which occur in the five different sections of the Mass. The discussion will be limited to the ordinary (the unchanging part) of the Mass, because those symbols belonging in the proper (which changes with feasts and seasons) will be considered in relation to the circle of the year in chapter nine. It will, of course, be impossible to treat all this rich symbolism in an exhaustive manner. The best we can hope to do is to open a few doors so that some readers will be able to walk into a new understanding of the holy reality of the Mass.

(i) *General view of Mass symbols*

Before we take each part separately, it will be well to have a preliminary notion about where we are going. We find that in the opening section of the Mass there is a profusion of symbols based on the four elements. One reason for this lavishness of symbolism is that the first section is especially the teaching part of the Mass, and the use of symbols from familiar concrete reality is an excellent teaching device.

The basic symbol here (which sets a pattern for the whole Mass) is that of the journey—around this main symbolic image cluster such other symbols as those of mountains, altar, and tabernacle of God; also the images of the lamb and the fruits of the earth (these last do not, however, appear until the second section of the Mass). Fire symbols occur several times, and water is implied in the baptismal references of Psalm 42. Unless we accept the singing and lamentations which float out on man's breath, there is no symbolism of air in this section.

The second section continues the journey symbol, but places even greater emphasis on the words gift, victim, sacrifice; and the main images are those of bread, wine, and altar for sacrifice. Fire and air symbols are also here, and there is water for symbolic cleansing in preparation for the sacrifice.

Sacrificial elements, among which we include the bread and wine of the Mass, are especially related to the fruitfulness of earth. This is because materials for sacrifice are, in every nation's worship, connected with life. Such materials are invariably fruits of earth or animals: things which have been alive and which serve as food to sustain life.

One reason for this is, of course, man's realization that his own life is his most valuable treasure, and therefore, wishing to give a good gift to his god (whatever god he believes in), he desires to offer himself—his very life. But he knows, too, that he is not lord of his own life, and so he cannot literally immolate himself to God. He therefore offers himself by means of symbols, which stand for his life.

The third section, the canon, has very little symbolism. It is almost pure statement, because here the greatest of all stories, that of our saving by Christ's passion, death, and resurrection, actually comes true in the telling. Here Christ is the true Paschal Lamb sacrificed for our reconciliation with his Father.

With the fourth section, the communion, begins a series of symbols related to the sharing of food: home, peaceful unity, a common meal. We know how men of all ages have felt that the sharing of a meal indicates a pledge of friendship. The whole famous Trojan war, for example, was fought not primarily because of the abduction of Helen of Troy, but rather because the man who stole her had violated the laws of hospitality by doing an injury to his host.

Our Lord makes specific mention of this belief in hospitality as a pledge of union and friendship when he says, speaking of Judas the traitor, "The man who shared my bread has lifted his heel to trip me up" (John 13:18). And here, moreover, Christ is quoting an ancient saying from the psalms: "The very man I trusted most . . . who shared my bread, has lifted his heel to trip me up" (Ps. 40:10). In many other places in folklore and in literature we find that the ideas of friendship and family solidarity are interlinked with the idea of shared bread. And this natural human symbolism enriches the significance of the Eucharist as a shared sacramental meal.

The last section of the Mass brings us back to the beginning, as we have said, by taking up the journey symbol and presenting it with a new meaning. We, as it were, receive our marching orders when the priest greets us with *"Ite, missa est*—Go, it is the dismissal." We might freely translate the phrase as: "Go, you are now sent out on a mission." For *missa* means *sent*—the words *mission, missile, missive,* come from the same stem. The whole Mass is a journey up to the mountain, to the altar of God, where we offer sacrifice to him. And at the end we are sent out on a different journey— a mission to carry the graces we have received at Mass into the everyday world.

(ii) *The journey symbol: especially Exodus*

The journey symbol is a very old and very natural one. And it is important in the Mass. Such symbolism of man's life as a journey runs through the literature of all ages. Homer and Virgil, for example, build their epics on stories of men's journeying toward a longed-for goal. Bunyan's *Pilgrim's Progress* pictures man the wayfarer seeking his home on the Celestial Mountain. Dante's *Divine Comedy* is a journey through hell, purgatory, and heaven—up to the vision of the Trinity itself.

Now as we have seen many times, and especially in the chapter on transfiguration, it is characteristic of Christ in his Church, to accept some material thing or some commonly held idea, to take into account its natural uses and meanings, and then by using it for his own purposes to transfigure it.

Probably the most famous of all journeys is that described in the book of Exodus. This natural symbol is first of all a historical story—the story of the journey of the Israelites to the promised land. But it further serves God's purpose by foreshadowing the journey of every man to his eternal goal, also the journey of humanity toward the days of salvation with the coming of the Redeemer, and finally the journey's end of the last days, when all the nations of the earth will come home to the promised land of eternity, and the mystical body of Christ will be complete. Then there will be "one Christ, loving himself" (as St. Augustine says).

Let us review the story of Exodus, pointing out some of its symbols, in order that we may see more clearly its relevance to the Mass. In the book we read that the Israelites had been many years in Egypt after Joseph had encouraged them to move to that land. Their nation had grown so prosperous that the Egyptians began to fear them. They were therefore enslaved and mistreated. Finally God raised up a leader,

Moses, who with his brother Aaron, was to rescue the people from slavery.

God appeared to Moses. He "revealed himself through a flame that rose up from the midst of a bush; . . . the bush was alight, yet did not burn" (Ex. 3:2). Here the Lord told him to ask Pharaoh if the Israelites might go out on a three days' journey and offer sacrifice to their God. The ruler refused again and again to let them go. And each time God sent a plague (of locusts, of frogs, of sickness) on Egypt. Every time, the message God told Moses to deliver was "Let my people go and offer me sacrifice" (Ex. 8:1, 8:20, and other places). Always Pharaoh refused.

The last plague was the worst of all. Moses told Pharaoh about it in these words: "The Lord sends you this message: At midnight I will make my way through the midst of Egypt, and with that every first-born thing in the land of Egypt shall die. . . . All over the land there shall be lament, such as never was yet . . . But where the Israelites dwell, all shall be still, man and beast, not a dog shall howl" (Ex. 11:4-7).

Then Moses instructed the Israelites (Ex. 12) that each household, on a certain day, was to choose a male yearling lamb, with no blemish on it, and immolate it. They were to smear some of its blood on their doorways, and roast the lamb. Then all were to eat it, with unleavened bread and wild herbs, in a sacrificial meal. This meal was to be eaten in haste, and all were to be prepared to begin a journey. This, he said, "is the night of the Pasch, the Lord's passing by." (Later on, God told the Israelites to repeat this ceremony yearly in remembrance of their deliverance.)

The blood of the lamb which marked their doorposts was to be a signal to the destroying angel, who when he saw this mark would spare the Hebrew children from death. All happened as Moses described it.

After this calamity, the Egyptians allowed the Israelites to leave the country, and they began their exodus from Egypt that very night. Now, however, "Pharao and his servants changed their minds about the Israelites. . . . So Pharao harnessed his chariot and took all his troops with him. . . . What fear fell upon the Israelites . . . when they looked around . . . and saw the Egyptians close behind them" (Ex. 14:5 ff.).

Then the Lord told Moses to lift his staff and "stretch out [his] hand over the sea, parting it this way and that, so that the Israelites [could] walk through the midst of the sea dryshod. . . . Vain the chariot, vain the horseman; I will teach the Egyptians to know me for what I am" (Ex. 14:16-19).

"So the Israelites went through the midst of the sea dryshod, with its waters towering up like a wall right and left" (Ex. 14:22). Then when the Egyptian pursuers pressed on after them into the sea, Moses, by God's command, "stretched out his hand towards the sea, [and] it went back to its bed. . . . Back came the water, overwhelming all the chariots and horsemen . . . so the Lord rescued Israel" (Ex. 14:27-30).

Then in a song of victory, the Israelites rejoiced that all those who threatened them "must watch . . . thy ransomed people go by unharmed. Passage thy people . . . have, and a home on the mountain thou claimest for thy own, the inviolable dwelling place, Lord, thou hast made for thyself" (Ex. 15:16-18).

So far we have seen a number of meaningful happenings which, as the story was later told repeatedly through the centuries, gathered ever greater significance. Now, in our time we see these same happenings signified, and their prophetic meaning fulfilled, in the symbolism of the Mass.

Some of these symbols are those of journeys out of slavery into freedom. The first epochal journey was begun in the sign of the paschal lamb. It continued in an escape from the pursuers through the waters—waters which were life to the Israelites but death to the enemy. The reason which God gave for the journey was that the Israelites might freely offer sacrifice to him. In the quotations we see also a foreshadowing of the fact that God was to appear to them on a mountain —Mount Sinai, which will be discussed below. And finally, we find that when the people came to the promised land they were to build a tabernacle for the Lord and offer him sacrifice on the holy hill of Jerusalem.

Other incidents having to do with water also occur on the journey. It is to be expected, of course, that the people should be much concerned about water since they were travelling in a desert country. Water was, therefore, important on the purely natural level. But besides this, the sign of water was one which God employed a number of times to show his care for them. After bringing the Israelites safely through the Red Sea waters into freedom, we find that God immediately works another kind of miracle—a sign in water.

This time the people "found no water in three days marching. So they came to Mara, and even here they could not drink the water" (Ex. 15:23) for it was bitter. The people complained. Then Moses cried out to the Lord, and the Lord "showed him a tree whose wood turned the waters sweet when it was thrown into them (Ex. 15:25). This wood is like the wood of the cross which we commemorate in the Mass—that wood which sweetened for us the bitter waters of death, by the redemption which Christ wrought. Then again when the people lacked water, the Lord told Moses to strike the rock and water would flow forth (Ex. 17:7). And so it happened.

Moreover, it was not only by water, but also in the sign of bread that God showed his providence towards his people. We have seen that the paschal feast was to be eaten with bread—bread prepared according to God's instructions. Now on the journey, when the people were hungry, the Lord rained down bread from heaven. And the "Israelites fed on this manna [this bread] for forty years" (Ex. 16:35).

In fire and a cloud, also, God showed his providence, for he went before them "to guide them on their journey; by day in a pillar of cloud, by night in a pillar of fire; he was their guide at all times" (Ex. 13:21).

Finally, the last incident which we shall describe here is that of the giving of the law on Mount Sinai. It was a scene full of awe. God began his instructions with a sentence about his people being a "royal priesthood, a consecrated nation" (Ex. 19:6)—phrases which St. Peter (I Pet. 2:9) was later to use in reference to the Christians—the new people of God. We read: "Moses went up to meet God, and the voice of God came to him from the mountain What shall be thy message to . . . Israel . . . ? Tell them, You have seen for yourselves . . . I carried you as if on eagle's wings. . . . You shall serve me as a royal priesthood, as a consecrated nation" (Ex. 19:4-6).

Then the people were told to wash their clothes and be ready. No one was to go near the mountain. And when the third day came, "morning broke, and all at once thunder was heard, lightning shone out, and the mountain was covered with thick mist [then] the whole of Mount Sinai was . . . wreathed in smoke, where the Lord had come down with fire about him" (Ex. 19:16-18).

Here the Lord gave his people the law they were to live by. So also in the Mass, as from his holy mountain, God speaks to us and tells us what we are to do to honor him and remain in his friendship. Then at the end of Exodus, while the people were still wandering in the desert, God laid down specific rules about the way they were to worship him. They were to build a tabernacle and carry it with them. This would be his dwelling place. Certain materials were to be used for it, and he even prescribed the exact ingredients of the incense they were to use in honoring him.

Fire and water, therefore, clouds in the air and incense, mountains and journeys on the earth—all the elements and their symbols come into this story. And all of them appear in the Mass. Moreover, just as we see the exodus of the Israelites from Egypt as a wayfaring out of slavery into freedom, and a search for the promised land, so also we see the journey as the underlying and unifying symbol in the Mass. Seeing these things, we realize that the Mass commemorates and furthers our own journey out of slavery to evil into the freedom of the children of God—his sons who are tending towards the promised land of our transfiguration in Christ.

That this taking of the Old Testament, and especially Exodus, as highly meaningful for Christianity is not farfetched, may be seen in several places in the New Testament. St. Stephen, for example, in Acts 17, gives his judges a résumé of the Old Testament, and dwells at length on the happenings in Exodus. In doing this he is trying to show them that Christianity is the fulfillment of these prophetic incidents and symbols.

St. Paul, too, reviews the story in Hebrews, Chapters 11 and 12. He says in one place, "What is the scene now of your approach to God? It is no longer a mountain that can be discerned by touch; no longer burning fire, and whirlwind, and darkness, and storm" (Heb. 12:18). No, but the "scene of your approach now is Mount Sion, is the heavenly Jerusalem, city of the living God; . . . Here is Jesus, the spokesman of the new covenant, and the sprinkling of his blood [at the paschal meal of the last supper, on Calvary, in the Mass], which has better things to say than Abel's (Heb. 12:22-24).

Abel's blood, of course, cried out for vengeance. Paul, here, is talking of the sprinkling of the paschal lamb's blood which was a mark of salvation of the Israelites. He is comparing this to the blood of Christ. He says that Christ's blood cries out for mercy as the paschal lamb's did—not for vengeance, like that of Abel who (Genesis 4) was killed by his brother. This whole epistle to the Hebrews, in fact, has for its main purpose to show the way the Old Testament is fulfilled in Christianity.

3. Parts of the Mass and symbolic images

What, then, could be more natural than that the paschal sacrifice of the new law should be filled with Old Testament symbols. In the Mass are symbols which come from the Bible, and which at the same time are natural images taken from the four elements. Some of these are: earth symbols of journeys, mountains, the lamb, the sign of bread; water symbols signifying cleansing and fructifying action; fire symbols, and air symbols of clouds and incense rising in the air as a sign of worship. All of them are not from the book of Exodus, but a great many are, as we shall see.

(i) *The symbols of the Fore-Mass*

The opening psalm of the Mass begins with the Exodus symbolism. We say, "I will go up to the altar of God." I will go—I will begin my journey. This journey will be a progress up a mountain to offer sacrifice to God. The offering of sacrifice on mountains is a prominent feature of the whole Old Testament: Noah gives thanks for his rescue from the flood on Mount Ararat; Abraham prepares to offer the sacrifice of his son Isaac on a mountain, and all through Exodus we follow descriptions of this practice.

After each of these sacrifices, a new life begins for the people concerned: Noah and his family settle down upon the land which has gone into a death by waters and is now made new; Abraham becomes the father of a new nation—the people of God; the Israelites come into a new life of freedom after the sacrifices they have offered in the desert, on the mountains, and especially after the sacrifice of the paschal lamb.

Such a note of rebirth, of new life, occurs very early in the Mass with the words: "I will go . . . to God, the giver of youth and happiness." This youth and happiness which God has given, and which he continually renews in the Mass, is the baptismal sharing in the divine life. By it we were made children of God, people of God. By it we received freedom from the Egypt of Satan's kingdom, and were given power to worship God "on his holy mountain" (Ps. 98:9), at his altar, in the Mass.

Because Baptism gave us a new life which is a share in the life of Christ and in the priesthood of Christ, therefore we are invested with power to do the action of the Mass. And this action essentially consists in our offering Christ to his Father after he has been brought within our reach by the consecrating words of the priest.

This first psalm in the Mass (Ps. 42) was, moreover, once sung by the newly baptized Christians as they came in procession to offer their first Mass. They had come on a journey through the dark waters of death to self and sin, into the life and light of Christ.

We, too, have made this journey into the dark valley, through the dark waters. As St. Paul insists: "You know well enough that we who were taken up into Christ by baptism have been taken up, all of us, into his death. In our baptism, we have been buried with him, died like him, that so, just as Christ was raised up by his Father's power from the dead, we too might live and move in a new kind of existence. We have to be closely fitted into the pattern of his resurrection. . . . The life he now lives is a life that looks towards God. And you, too, must think of yourselves as dead to sin, and alive with a life that looks towards God . . ." (Rom. 6:3 ff.). We have been plunged into the passion and death of Christ and have emerged as new men—men given "youth and happiness," men able to "go up to the altar of God."

Further on in Psalm 42, the Exodus symbols become even more prominent. The priest says, "The light of thy presence, the fulfillment of thy promise, let these be my escort, bringing me safe to thy holy mountain, to the tabernacle where thou dwellest." By the mention of the "light of thy presence . . . my escort" we are reminded of the pillar of fire which went before God's people, guiding them out of captivity, across the desert to the promised land, where they would be able freely and fittingly to offer sacrifice to their God.

The promised land is also suggested by the words "safe to thy holy mountain where thou dwellest." When the Israelites came to the promised land, they had come home. There they were able to build a temple ("the tabernacle where thou dwellest") for the offering of sacrifice to God on the holy hill of Jerusalem. This is why they could exclaim: "The Lord is great, great honour is his due here in the city where he, our God, dwells, here on his holy mountain. Boldly stands the hill of Sion, the pride of the whole earth, where it slopes northward . . . within those walls, God is made known in his protecting care" (Ps. 47:1-4).

In Christianity, moreover, mountains are used as symbols for Christ. For example, on the feast of St. Catherine, November 25, we find Mount Sinai linked symbolically with Christ. Here is the prayer from the Mass: "O God, who gavest the law to Moses on the summit of Mount Sinai . . . we pray thee grant that [St. Catherine's] pleading may enable us to reach the mountain which is Christ."

The reason behind the symbolism may be that Christ, having a human nature, is like the mountain, one with the earth, sharing in its materials; but being also divine, he is, again like the mountain, raised high above the earth. When we human beings look up at a mountain we are humbled by its majesty. We feel small. And just so, we look up at God, made a human being like us, and we are filled with reverence.

But on the other hand when we stand on a mountain, we lose our small selves in the expanded vision—we feel freed, released from the confining cage of self. And this expanded vision is also a result of our looking at temporal things from the height of the mountain which is Christ. When we adopt his vision of things, when we stand on his high mountain, then we feel "time ravel thin about us" (as Eunice Tietjens says in the poem quoted earlier), and we know a "swift, white peace, a presence manifest."

The mountain, then, both humbles and exalts us. But most important of all here, it furnishes us a place in which to hear what God would tell us (for in the Mass he speaks, as he did on Sinai), and a place where we can offer sacrifice to him. For the altar is our mountain of sacrifice. And here we offer God the Lamb of the New Covenant, Christ our Lord.

Finally, in this psalm, we are led by the words, "To the tabernacle where thou dwellest" to think not only of the temple of Jerusalem, but of all the shelters on earth, especially the places of worship, and of that special temple of God which is built in human souls: "Do you not understand that you are God's temple, and that God's Spirit has his dwelling in you? . . . It is a holy thing, this temple of God which is nothing other than yourselves" (I Cor. 3:16). And again, it is through baptism that we are thus made temples of God.

From the above analysis, it can be seen that the whole of Psalm 42 is informed with a submerged baptismal symbolism, and therefore it suggests insistently the symbolic meaning of water. Many highly significant incidents having to do with water were seen above in our review of Exodus. We mentioned, for example, the time when Moses caused water to flow for the thirsting people from a rock, and the other time when God showed Moses a tree whose wood had power to sweeten bitter waters. These traditions as well as many others found in the Old Testament are implicit in the references to water which are found in the Mass. And so we, too, like the Israelites, are saved, and given strength, and refreshed for our journey by waters—the waters which flow to us from Christ.

After Psalm 42, the words, "I will go up to the altar of God, to God the giver of youth and happiness" are repeated. In this way the symbols of journey, mountain, altar, new life, are all gathered together. After this comes the *confiteor*, in which we ask to be cleansed from our sins, and then another reference to our rebirth in Christ: "Thou wilt relent, O God, and *bring us to life.*"

Next the cleansing qualities associated with water as well as the symbols of shelter appear once more. They are apparent in: "Take away from us our iniquities . . . so that with souls made clean, we may be . . . worthy to enter the holy of holies"—which is God's tabernacle, his dwelling place.

When we come to the *Gloria* we find that the symbolism jumps over many centuries. It is the property of symbols to disregard chronology, to move about in the ages with freedom. Here, therefore, we think of the light which shone from the skies, and the star which appeared on the first Christmas night when the angels sang this song.

Exodus is, however, not forgotten even here, for in the prayer we find that Christ is referred to as the Lamb of God. This Lamb of God is going up to the altar of sacrifice during Mass, to take away the sins of the world. He is the Paschal Lamb whose blood means salvation for God's people. He is also that "Lamb standing upright, yet slain . . . in sacrifice" which appears in St. John's book of revelations (Apoc. 5:6).

This is true because with the Mass, the Son of God who suffered for us, once more presents to his Father the marks of his death on the cross for us. He still, in heaven, bears the marks of this sacrificial death, and "lives on still to make intercession on our behalf" (Heb. 7:25).

This paschal lamb of Exodus was a sacrifice and a banquet —a meal and an instrument of salvation. Christ, too, is both of these things. And we shall find the phrase "Lamb of God" re-echoing in the preparation for the shared sacrificial meal at the communion of the Mass.

The symbol of fire appears twice more in the Fore-Mass. First, before the gospel the priest prays that God may use a fire (a live coal) to cleanse his lips before he proclaims the holy news of the gospel: "Cleanse my heart and my lips, almighty God, who didst cleanse the lips of the prophet Isaias with a live coal . . ." And then in the creed, fire appears as light when we call Christ "God from God, light from light." Now with the *Amen* at the end of the creed, the Fore-Mass, which is the preparation for the sacrifice proper, comes at an end.

(ii) *Symbols in the offertory*

The second section, the offertory, opens with the salutation *"Dominus vobiscum*—the Lord be with you," to which we answer, *"Et cum spiritu tuo*—and with you." This greeting reminds us once more that we are on a journey. It is like the farewell good wishes we find in different languages. In Spanish, for example, when someone is going away we say *"Adios,"* meaning, "Go with God." And the people of Africa speak the same way, "Go with God." Even our English *goodbye,* though we seldom think about it, means "God be with you." After this greeting, then, we continue on our journey "up to the altar of God."

With the offertory, a new thing becomes apparent. In the Fore-Mass we talked about symbols, but did not handle them. Now there is a direct contact, a handling of symbols of all four elements: the bread and wine of earth's fruitfulness, the water used to mingle with the wine, the air and fire of the incensing during high Mass.

The first thing the priest does during the offertory is to lift up the small plate with the bread for sacrifice on it. And in the accompanying prayer he reminds us once again of the paschal lamb, for he asks God to accept this "unblemished sacrificial offering." Now one of the rules God specifically laid down was that the paschal lamb "must be a male yearling lamb—with no blemish on it" (Ex. 12:5).

Next comes the beautiful prayer during the rite of the mingling of water and wine. The sacrificial and sacramental symbolism of this prayer was discussed in the chapter on Christ the center. Here, as we have seen before, we not only talk about symbols, but they are actually handled, for the priest pours a few drops of water (which here represents us, since it is of little worth compared to the more valuable wine) into the chalice of wine (representing Christ). He is preparing to offer this chalice as a part of our sacrifice, our gift to God.

On the symbolic level, bread and wine are especially fitted to represent man's life (which is here offered to God in symbol, as we have said). First of all, these things are nourishing —they support life. Then they are shaped by man's work. They have not been picked in the fields and offered immediately to God. They have, rather, been changed from their natural state: grown by man's industry, gathered from the fields, and transformed by man's skill from wheat and grapes to juice and flour and then to wine and bread.

All these changes in the natural product are brought about by man's artistry, hence these elements of bread and wine stand not only for his life of body and soul, but also for his specifically human qualities of intelligence and manual skill. Besides these facts, bread especially represents man's activity because its nourishment provides power for us to carry on life's activities.

Wine, on the other hand, while it too is nourishing, is also significant in two further directions. It is the chalice of suffering which Christ spoke of in his agony, and which comes to all human beings in some form. It is also a delightful and refreshing drink, and so stands for our joy. The things which happen to us, which we experience—sorrow and joy—are in this way symbolized by the wine, while the things we actually do, the activities of our deliberation, are indicated by the symbolism of bread.

Moreover, through these symbols, and in actual fact, we have been offering not only bread and wine, but also ourselves to God. When all these gifts are transformed by God's power, there is, however, one significant difference between the first two gifts and that of our human selves. The bread and wine, according to this interpretation, are wholly obedient. They lie wholly receptive before God. When, therefore, the moment of consecration comes, the whole substances of bread and wine will disappear, and the substance of the living Christ will be in them instead. The bread and wine will be totally changed into Christ.

But we too, are offered. We have also made a gift of ourselves. We, nevertheless, often put up barriers to God's invasion of our being. Thus it comes about that our transfiguration—our transformation into Christ—is only gradual. Just so much of our "substance"—our inner spiritual being—becomes "Christed" as we leave open to God's transfiguring action.

This is the reason that most of us participate in many Masses and yet come very slowly to appear in the image of Christ. Nevertheless it is true that after Mass each of us can say with continually increasing confidence: "I am alive; or rather, not I; it is Christ that lives in me" (Gal. 2:20). Dom Marmion, the great spiritual writer of our time, puts this thought well. He says: "Every morning I place myself on the paten with the host that is about to become Jesus Christ; and in the same way that Jesus is there to be eaten by all sorts of persons . . . so I am eaten all day long by all kind of people. May our dear Saviour be glorified by my destruction, as He is by His own immolation." [46]

Here Marmion is talking of both the sacrificial and sacramental aspects of the Mass. We can, like him, give all our time, all our energies to God, in order that he may change them into the time and the energies of Christ. Then, as Christ allows himself to be consumed by the human beings who come to receive Holy Communion, so we can allow our time to be devoted to the good of all who come demanding a share of our time and our activities.

After the mingling of the water and wine, the priest lifts up the chalice praying that the offering it contains may ascend with a sweet fragrance to God. Here we find an image from the element of air, for fragrance comes from perfume, from incense, which rises in air and becomes a part of it. We remember, too, that God told Moses how to make incense for his worship: "With all the perfumer's art . . . fit for hallowing. . . . This incense shall be all holiness; you must not compound it so for your own use, it is set apart for the Lord" (Ex. 30:37).

Next the prayer to the Holy Spirit is said: "Come, thou sanctifier . . . and bless these sacrificial gifts prepared for the glory of thy holy name." In meditating on this prayer we think of the Spirit who came at Pentecost in tongues of fire, and of the fact that the usual way of indicating that something is taken completely from the use of man and given to God is by fire. We read continually in the Old Testament, for example, that the sacrifices were to be consumed by fire. This total annihilation of something is one reason for the use of fire in sacrificing. Another is, perhaps, the fact that smoke rises to heaven—a symbol of the glory to be given to God by this gift is rising to him.

Following this prayer, if it is a high Mass that is being offered, there comes the incensing of the altar. Incense, like fire, symbolizes our worship as it rises to God. The smoke, moreover, comes from fire—from the burning coals on which the incense is placed. And the prayers here also clarify the symbolism of air and fire: "Lord, let this incense rise to thee, and bring down upon us thy mercy." "Welcome as incense-smoke let my prayer rise up before thee, Lord" (the latter prayer is taken from Psalm 140:2). These two phrases speak of the symbolism of air. The next one is related to fire: "May the Lord kindle within us the fire of his love, and the flame of everlasting charity."

Then another symbolic action takes place when the priest cleanses his hands in a little water while he prays Psalm 25, which mentions the beauty of the Lord's house (again the dwelling, tabernacle symbol), and the guidance of God needed for a journey: "Guide my steps clear of wrong . . . My feet are set on firm ground."

Now a prayer to the Trinity summarizes the content of the sacrifice about to be offered. It will be a gift made "in memory of the passion, resurrection, and ascension of our Lord Jesus Christ." It will be a re-presenting in our time and space of all these mysteries, these holy actions, of Christ.

Finally the priest turns to the people, calling on them to join closely in the sacrifice. He says: *"Orate, Fratres*—Pray, brethen, that my sacrifice and yours may prove acceptable in the eyes of God . . ." And the people answer, "May the Lord accept this sacrifice . . ." After this the priest says the secret prayers which summarize the petitions of all present. When they are concluded the people ratify the offertory and the action of the Mass thus far by saying, *"Amen*—we consent."

(iii) *Symbols in the Canon*

In beginning the third and central section of the Mass we again have the greeting for a journey: *Dominus vobiscum.* This is followed by a dialogue which urges us: "Lift up your hearts." "We have lifted them up." "Let us give thanks. . . ." "It is right and just."

From this time until we come to the communion, there are few earthly symbols, for this is a heavenly story, one which comes true in the telling. It is a heavenly drama which *happens* while it is being acted out. There are constant references throughout this part to offerings and sacrificial gifts. And just before the Consecration, the priest prays that our offering "may become for us the Body and Blood of thy dearly beloved Son, our Lord Jesus Christ." Here we are on a new level of reality higher than the purely symbolic.

Immediately after this, the priest changes his form of prayer from praise and petition addressed to God to the form of narration. He tells the story of the central event of the Last Supper. We remember that at this Supper Christ was celebrating the Paschal feast, the commemoration of the exodus from Egypt. Here is the actual story that comes true in the telling: "He, on the day before he suffered death, took bread into his holy and worshipful hands and lifting up his eyes to thee, God, his almighty Father in heaven, and giving thanks to thee, he blessed it, broke it, and gave it to his disciples saying: Take, all of you, and eat of this, FOR THIS IS MY BODY."

And again the priest narrates the manner in which Christ took "this goodly cup" into his hands and "blessed it, and gave it to his disciples saying: 'Take, all of you, and drink of this, FOR THIS IS THE CHALICE OF MY BLOOD, of the new and everlasting covenant, a mystery of faith. It shall be shed for you and many others, so that sins may be forgiven.' "

Finally, the narration quotes Christ's words, "Whenever you shall do these things, you shall do them in memory of me." By this saying, he told the disciples to continue doing this holy action, to continue offering the Mass. The Paschal Feast of the New Covenant is to be repeated, just as the Pasch of the Old Testament was to be renewed in ceremonial celebration.

After this, the priest takes up again the non-narratory prayers of praise and petition to God. He says two oblation prayers which make it clear that the gift we are now offering to God is more than our original present of ourselves and our bread and wine.

We are now offering "the passion, resurrection, and glorious ascension of Christ." We are giving to the Father "out of the gifts [he] has bestowed upon us, a sacrifice that is pure, holy, and unblemished." This is the "sacred Bread of everlasting life, and the Cup of eternal salvation."

In the second of these oblation prayers we memorialize all the sacrifices of former times, for these foreshadowed the one great Sacrifice, which is the Mass. We ask that God may accept this Bread and this Cup as he accepted the sacrifice of Abel (the son of Adam, who stands for all men before they were divided by creed or nation), the sacrifice of our father Abraham (who symbolizes the Israelites and their sacrifices), and "that which Melchisidech [a non-Jewish priest who offered bread and wine] sacrificed to thee, a holy offering, a victim without blemish."

Both of these oblation prayers contain the word "unblemished," which we have described as having relevance to the symbol of the paschal lamb, and to Christ as the Lamb of God.

Now we ask that God's holy angel may carry our gift "up to [his] altar on high, before the face of [his] divine majesty," so that those who share in the communion banquet may be "filled with every grace and heavenly blessing." In this prayer, all those who will receive holy communion at this Mass, are especially prayed for. We also pray for the dead who have gone before us with the "sign of faith" imprinted on them by baptism. We ask that they may come to a place of "cool repose, of light and peace"—that they may come into the promised land with its brightness and cool air (fire and air symbols).

At last we pray that we ourselves may have part and fellowship with the family of apostles and martyrs. Then we are ready for the prayer of praise which concludes the canon.

This prayer gives thanks that "all these good gifts"—the gift of Christ himself first, and then earth, air, fire, water, in all their meanings—come to us through the mediation of Christ. And we say that it is also "through him, and with him, and in him," that the Father and the Spirit have all honor and glory. "World without end." Then all answer the important *Amen* which closes the canon, and by which we signify our assent to the sacrificial action in which we have been engaged.

(iv). *Symbols in the communion*

Now with the two-line preparation for the Lord's prayer which was described earlier, we begin the fourth section of the Mass, that of the communion. This part is marked by symbols of hospitality, home, food; and its keynote is *peace*. The *Pater Noster* (Our Father) begins the pattern with its petition for our daily bread. And the prayer following it asks for peace.

The concept of peace strengthens the symbolism of bread in two ways. First, as we have explained above, the eating of a meal together has in all ages and all countries been taken as a sign of concord and peace. And second, in the appearance of Christ after his resurrection, he nearly always did two things: he wished peace to his friends, and he ate with them or gave them something to eat. We see him, for example, consenting to come in with the two disciples at Emmaus. "And then, when he sat down at table with them, he took bread, and blessed, and broke it, and offered it to them; whereupon . . . they recognized him" (Luke 24:30-31).

Then there is the time our Lord stood and ate before the apostles to convince them that he was truly risen and present, body and soul. Luke tells us: "Then, while they were still doubtful, and bewildered with joy, he asked them Have you anything here to eat? So they put before him a piece of roast fish, and a honeycomb; and he took these and ate in their presence and shared his meal with them" (Luke 24:41-43).

And for a final example there is the appealing picture at the sea of Tiberias, when the apostles came ashore after a night's fishing and found their breakfast prepared by the risen Lord himself: "So they went ashore, and found a charcoal fire made there, with fish and bread cooking on it. Bring some of the fish you have just caught, Jesus said. . . . Come and break your fast. . . . So Jesus came up and took bread which he gave to them, and fish as well" (John 21:9 ff.).

He not only ate with them, but as we have said, his constant greeting especially during these days was: "Peace be upon you; it is myself, do not be afraid" (Luke 24:36). In this way he links together the two ideas of food and peace, and these two are also linked during the preparation for communion in the Mass.

During these days when he has no need of food at all, Christ is more concerned with it than we have yet seen him. In this way, perhaps, he was not only proving that he still had a human body, but he was also indirectly reminding his friends of the last momentous meal they had eaten with him on the night before he died.

At this meal too the sharing of bread was significant of peace and unity: "Peace is my bequest to you, and the peace which I give you is mine to give" (John 14:27); "He who loves me will win my Father's love, and I too will love him" (John 14:21); "I have given them the privilege . . . that they should all be one, as we are one" (John 18:22); "I have longed and longed to share this paschal meal with you" (Luke 22:15).

The greeting which comes next in the Mass is a modification of the usual *Dominus vobiscum*. This time, in line with what has just been said, it is a wish for our peace: "The peace of the Lord be always with you," says the priest. And after that we have the prayer: "May this mingling and hallowing of the body and blood of our Lord Jesus Christ," which we will receive as food, "be for us who receive it a source of eternal life." We see here the uniting of the three ideas of food, of peace, and of life.

Now come three invocations to the Lamb of God—the paschal lamb, the Lamb of the Apocalypse "standing upright, yet slain . . . in sacrifice" (5:6). This second lamb is Christ as he now lives in glory, bearing in his body the marks of the sacrificial death he suffered for us.

The third of these invocations to the Lamb of God also asks especially for peace: "Lamb of God, who takest away the sins of the world [here and now by the sacrifice of the Mass], give us peace."

The next three prayers are a direct preparation for holy communion, and the first of these repeats three times the word peace. The second asks that we never be separated from God—a prayer for unity. And the third prays that the "partaking [as food] of thy Body, Lord, [may] be . . . a safeguard of body and mind." Peace, unity, food, the three themes are clear in the three prayers.

Now the priest announces, "I will take the Bread of Heaven," and while holding the consecrated Bread in his hands he says the prayer of the centurion to Christ—a prayer which implies hospitality and welcome: "Lord, I am not worthy that thou shouldst enter *beneath my roof*." It is as if he would say, I know my home is not good enough for you to come in and visit, but please come anyway. Your power can make it more worthy: "Say only the word, and my soul shall be healed."

In rapid succession after this we find references to the Body of our Lord (which is our Food), the chalice of salvation, the Blood of our Lord Jesus Christ. And then holding up the consecrated Host in view of the people, the priest uses for the fifth time in the Mass, the phrase, *Lamb of God*. He says, in John the Baptist's words: "Behold the Lamb of God, behold him who takes away the sins of the world." Then the people come up to receive holy communion while the priest repeats for them the words: "Lord, I am not worthy."

After the sacrificial banquet has taken place, the symbol of food is repeated in two prayers filled with compressed meaning. First, is said a prayer structured like an equation: "That which our mouths have taken, Lord, may we possess in purity of mind; and may the gift of the moment become for us an everlasting remedy." The thought is: May the holy Food received into our bodies, be to our minds, as this transitory gift of the Holy Sacrament, becomes for us everlasting in effect. The equation, then, is: food for bodies is to minds as transitory gift is to everlasting life. The physical is to the spiritual as the temporal is to the eternal.

Secondly, comes a further reference to food, in a prayer which asks that the effects of this holy nourishment may be felt in all our being: "May thy Body, Lord, which I have taken, and thy Blood which I have drunk, cleave to every fiber of my being. Grant that no stain of sin may be left in me, now that I am renewed by this pure and holy sacrament."

Following these prayers of thanksgiving after the sacred banquet, are the postcommunion prayers which are like the collects in summarizing the intentions of the people, and in being changeable with the day's feasts. These prayers end with our communal word of consent and ratification: *Amen.*

(v) *Symbols in the closing section*

The fifth and last section of the Mass, which is a closing conversation, as the Fore-Mass was an opening conversation, echoes the first section's three symbols of the journey ("Ite, missa est"), the altar ("offered in the sight of thy divine majesty"), and light ("He was the true light"). It begins with the greeting we have grown to expect: "The Lord be with you."

This injunction with its meaning of "Go with God," is reinforced by the words which inaugurate another, different journey from the one we have been engaged on up to now. The priest says, "Ite, missa est." In effect, this may mean: Go, you are sent out with work to do and strength gained from the Mass will help you do it. We have, so far, been on a journey "to the altar of God." Now our journey will take us into the daily world to carry there the fruits of our Mass.

After the greeting and the dismissal, there is still some farewell conversation between us and God. From the customs we find in human farewells, we should expect just this pause for a final few words. First in a summary prayer, we ask that the Holy Trinity may be pleased with our offered gifts. And then the priest gives us God's answer, for in token of God's pleasure, he blesses us in the name of the Trinity: Father, Son, and Holy Spirit.

Then God speaks to us in the last gospel, which gives us his final word. In it once more all of creation is brought together—all the things we have been finding in the Mass—in Christ. For as St. John says here, "it was through Him that all things came into being." This echoes the prayer at the end of the canon: "It is ever through him that all these good things are . . . endowed with life . . . and bestowed upon us." We are reminded once more, by this, of all the references we have found to that new life which is the gift of Christianity: "In him there was life, and that life was the light of men."

"He came to what was his own, and they who were his own gave him no welcome," the gospel continues. And those who are at Mass realize that their own hospitality has been extended to Christ. They are not like the ones who "gave him no welcome." When we have said, "Lord, I am not worthy," our only concern has been lest our hospitality should not be fitting for such a guest.

Then we see the baptismal symbolism repeated in the phrase, "All those who did welcome him he empowered to become the children of God." Hearing this, we remember that the essence of the baptismal happening is our reception of a new life which makes us children of God in truth.

Finally, the last sentence of the Mass sums up all that we have been saying about the earthliness of God's ways with man, for here we find John's clear statement that the Word not only was with the Father, delighting in creation, in the days of Genesis, but the Word also took to himself a created body, made of elements like ours: "And the Word was made flesh and came to dwell among us"—"He pitched his tent among us" as the Kleist and Lilly translation of the gospels puts it (Bruce, 1954). And in both translations are words which signify the earth-symbolism of dwelling places.

We realize, moreover, that now since the Word has been made flesh, we have had sight of his glory, "glory such as belongs to the Father's only begotten Son, full of grace and truth." Because of this thought, our minds turn back once more to the Christmas Mass which says, "Through the mystery of the Word made flesh, thy splendour has shone before our eyes with a new radiance." And looking back, now, over the journey we have made, we find ourselves ready to travel forward into the world of every day, strong with new strength, and we conclude the Mass with our expression of gratitude: *"Deo gratias*—Thanks be to God."

Much more could be said about the Mass, but we have seen enough to realize that many of its symbols are related to those in the book of Exodus, and that in it we find earth, air, fire, and water invested with new significance and new power. It is now time to consider the second great circle, that of the sacraments, where the mysteries of Christ which have been actualized here in the Mass, flow out to meet the specific needs of every man.

CHAPTER SEVEN

Of the Sacraments: Second Circle

> The beloved people has a God great as no other; he rides in heaven to deliver thee, the clouds making way for his majestic coming; there, on high, is his dwelling, and yet the eternal arms reach down to uphold thee.
>
> *Deut.* 33:26

THE MASS, as we have seen, is one kind of circle. Now we come to another kind—that shaped by the revolving movement of time. Of these rings of time, the first one we will discuss is the circle of man's life.

Our life is a circle which comes out from God, grows to a rounded whole, and returns to God to find fulfillment. Within this circle, this rounded progression of beginning, increase, and return, we live through a recurrent yet varied pattern of days, weeks, and years. In living out this cycle, moreover, we have certain basic needs, and these are related, as we shall see, in many ways to the four elements of earth, air, fire, water. The same needs occur in both natural and supernatural realms of life, and in both realms the four elements function to mean something; that is, to have significance; and to do something, that is, to have power.

These basic needs exist, first of all on the natural level,

that of our psycho-physical being. If we are to live, for example, we must first be born. This is to say that we must come into existence as human beings. After this, we need to be nourished, to be given food which sustains life and furnishes energy. When our needs are fulfilled, we receive not only physical strength, but a sense of psychological security. All these needs and their satisfactions reverberate on psychological as well as physical levels.

Besides needing food for life, we also need to grow to maturity, to become independent, to be able to fend for ourselves, and at the same time to shoulder some responsibility toward others. When we have become adults we need to be invested with the power to bring other human beings into life, because for full maturity one should be capable of parenthood.

Again, one of our psychological needs is what we might call sociality. It means that man is by nature a social being, and therefore he has a need for other human beings. This craving is satisfied when we share food at a common table, when human beings take each other to have and to hold in marriage, and in many other ways.

One social function of others in our regard is, at times, to help us to judge our own actions, to encourage us in good, and show us how to undo the wrongs we have committed against ourselves or others. This can take place in the conversation of friend and friend, in the training of children by parents or teachers, and most formally, in courts of law.

Then if we become ill, we need healing and help for our ailing bodies and distressed minds. As we know, illness is of the mind as well as of the body, and so those who would heal bodies need to concern themselves also with minds. Again this is but one of the functions of man's sharing in social life —he finds others who help to set his mind at rest, who give new courage to his faltering will, and in doing these things, they aid in healing his body as well as his soul.

And finally when our cycle of life is completed, our body is ready to return to its origins, the elements—as the Ash Wednesday liturgy reminds us: "Dust thou art and unto dust shalt thou return" (Gen. 3:19). And in the meantime our immortal soul, if it be ready for its normal fulfillment, returns to God, its true home, and there awaits its final reunion with the body. As the creed says in triumphant tones: *"Expecto—*I expect the resurrection of the dead and life everlasting."

In all this cycle of life there is a unified movement from a beginning, through growth to maturity and full flowering of powers, to the final coming to rest and completion.

From one point of view, each life is different from all others, and within each life the days and years are infinitely varied. Yet each day moves from dawn to dusk, through dark to dawn again, in what Dylan Thomas calls "the adventure of the coming and going of simple night and day." [47] Each week circles from Sunday, through weekdays, to Sunday again, until once more the Sabbath rings "slowly in the pebbles of the holy streams," in the same poet's words.

Then, too, each year moves through its seasons with regularity and patterned order, "with slow rotation suggesting permanence" (as Eliot says), but with endless variation, too. Is any spring ever like the last one? Or any red-gold autumn ever the same as last year's?

Each of us, moreover, as we live out our cycle of days, is sustained, modified, terrified, and solaced by earth, air, fire, and water. A consciousness, therefore, of these elements which concern us so nearly can unify and enrich man's life even on the purely natural level.

On the supernatural level, this same cycle of life is to be seen, with its unity and patterned recurrence made vivid with variety because of our changing responses to God and to people, and our varied contacts with the four elements.

Here all these details of life are transfigured by being invested with significance and efficacy for man's transformation into the likeness of Christ. These transfigurations come about because the sacramental and sacrificial power of God works in and through men's actions and material things.

At baptism we begin our life's cycle by being cleansed and "born anew . . . from water, and from the Holy Spirit" (John 3:3, 5), as Christ said to Nicodemus. Then we are nourished by the Eucharist, and brought to an age of responsibility by confirmation. In the sacrament of penance, we are judged by God's representative who brings us the divine forgiveness for our wrongdoing and appoints for us ways of making reparation.

Then our ability to hand on life to others on the natural level is consecrated through matrimony. And man is empowered to share life on the supernatural level through the sacrament of orders.

When we become ill physically and weak spiritually our soul and body are given peace and healing by the anointing of all our senses—those five senses whose good use fills us with gladness and holiness all our life long. If this illness is the one which is to complete the cycle of our earthly life, we are made ready by this sacrament of anointing to step into our fulfillment—to come at last to the answer given man's deepest yearning for happiness in the beatific vision. This readiness becomes ours through the power of that anointing unto glory (as St. Thomas calls it) which we name extreme unction—the last anointing.

Let us summarize now: baptism is a cleansing and a rebirth; confirmation, an anointing which brings our powers to maturity. Holy Eucharist is our soul's food. Penance is a judgment and tribunal for forgiveness. Matrimony is a contract entered into by two persons with the giving of life to new human beings—new potential members for the kingdom of God—as its primary end. Holy orders is the investing of men with power to give supernatural life and do all things necessary to sustain that life in others. Extreme unction is an anointing destined to heal body and soul, or to make the soul ready to step into the vision of God.

Scattered about among these great sacraments, and touching every detail of our lives are hundreds of little sacraments which we call sacramentals. By the blessing of children and of water, of fields and homes and food, of candles and bonfires, of automobiles and typewriters, all the things that man loves or uses are sanctified and given power to aid in his transfiguration into the likeness of Christ.

Let us look at a few of these blessings.[48] Here is the blessing for a bonfire:

> O Lord God, Father almighty, unfailing Ray and Source of all light, sanctify this new fire, and grant that after the darkness of this life we may come unsullied to thee Who art Light eternal.

This prayer is part of a very ancient tradition—the blessing of bonfires on the vigil of St. John the Baptist's feast. It is symbolic of the fact that John gave testimony of the true light which is Christ.

The blessing of the meat of a lamb is reminiscent of Exodus:

> O God, who by thy servant Moses didst command thy people in their deliverance from Egypt to kill a lamb in symbol of Jesus Christ, our Lord, and didst prescribe that its blood be used to anoint their doorposts, do thou bless and sanctify this flesh which we thy servants wish to eat in praise of thee.

Here we find reference to Moses, the leader of the Israelites on their journey, and also the explicit relating of the paschal lamb to Christ.

Now let us look at the blessing of an automobile with its reminder of a story from the Acts of the Apostles:

> . . . O Lord God . . . with thy holy hand bless this vehicle. Appoint . . . thy holy angels, ever to guard and keep safe

from danger them that ride herein. And as by thy Levite, Philip, thou didst bestow faith and grace upon the Ethiopian, seated in his carriage, and reading Holy Writ, so likewise show the way of salvation to thy servants . . .

Two things necessary for those who ride in cars are prayed for here—to be safe from danger, and to find the right road. The story behind the blessing is that Philip came upon a man riding along in his carriage and reading the prophets aloud to himself. Philip came up and asked him if he understood what the prophecies meant. He said that he could not understand them unless someone explained them to him. Philip offered to do this, and the outcome of the story was that the man believed in Christ, foretold by the prophets, and was baptized immediately.

In all these blessings, no animate or inanimate being is excluded. The prayers of the rites are full of meaning and beauty, and will richly repay one who meditates on them. They might be used informally by any member of the family to pray for God's blessings, even though it is the priest's special power to call down God's sacramental consecration. It would be fascinating to make a study of some of them, but this cannot be done here. We must turn now to the sacraments themselves. In the discussion it will be helpful to have the actual texts of the sacraments at hand.[49]

In our discussion we shall point out the structure or design of action in each sacrament and comment on the symbolism of the four elements as it occurs. Though it would be profitable to study each prayer used, this cannot be done now. We shall, therefore, analyze these beautiful prayers only in instances where such analysis is needed to explain structure and symbols.

At baptism, as we have said, we are born into supernatural life, and our cycle begins. It is interesting to note in passing that the end of the cycle (as one would expect of circular structure) is implicit in the beginning. For example, one of the first prayers the priest says for the person being baptized is: May he come to the glory destined for those who are born anew.

This points to the fact that the purpose of baptism is to begin the preparation of the human soul for its final goal which is glory—a transfiguration which will empower the Christian to share in God's eternal happiness. This is the process which is completed and rounded out in the final anointing. That anointing puts the finishing touches on the mystery of life and growth which was begun at baptism. In the degree to which this divine life, during our years on earth, invades our being, to that degree will we have capacity to rejoice when we come at last to the place of refreshment, light, and peace which every Mass asks for us.

1. *Baptism:* "Unless a man be born again . . ."

This first of the sacraments, baptism, can be seen as structured in five parts, much as we have seen the Mass to be designed. According to this scheme, the first and last sections of the ceremony are largely composed of speech, and the middle three are mainly action. The center section contains the essence of the sacrament, while the first and second are preparation, and the fourth and fifth follow as results from the central action. Symbols from the four elements are important throughout.

A dialogue, therefore, with some exchange of actions constitutes the material of the first section. Here the Church, through her minister the priest, speaks to and with the candidate for baptism. The priest asks what the candidate desires from the Church of God, and he discovers that faith and everlasting life are the gifts sought.

This life everlasting is not something exclusively reserved for heaven, but a reality which will begin this very day of the baptism and (in the faithful Christian) will grow continually richer until the day of his entrance into glory.

Next the priest instructs the candidate about the duties involved in his profession as a Christian. Afterwards, employing the Holy Spirit's symbol of air (breath, wind) he breathes upon the candidate and says, "Depart from him, unclean spirit, and give place to the Holy Spirit." This action is like that of our Lord when he appeared to his disciples after the resurrection: then "he breathed on them, and said to them, Receive the Holy Spirit" (John 20:23). Then, too, it was with a sound like "that of a strong wind blowing" that the Spirit came at Pentecost (Acts 2:2).

In the baptismal ceremony, this is the first of a series of exorcisms which give the impression of a mighty struggle being waged for the possession of this human soul. By this breathing, the evil spirit begins to find his hold loosened, and the wind of the Holy Spirit begins to effect the sanctification of the soul.

The priest then marks the candidate with the sign of the cross—a symbol of Christ's proprietorship—and prays that all the snares of Satan in which he may have become entangled, may be broken, and that the gate of God's fatherly love may be opened to receive the candidate.

Next comes the blessing of the "creature salt"—the salt which signifies wisdom—and the placing of a few grains of it on the candidate's tongue. Salt is a mineral taken from the earth, and so is related to the first of the four elements. It is called the salt of wisdom, because wisdom is especially a taste —a savoring of God's mysteries. We are furthermore reminded that Christ called his disciples the salt of the earth, and he warned them to beware lest they lose their savor—lest they become what Hopkins calls "spendsavour salt." He said they were rather to preserve, as salt preserves, the holiness of their calling (Matt. 5:13).

Besides this, the salt is also to function as a kind of appetizer, a preparation for the Eucharistic banquet. According to the words of the rite, the candidate is not to "hunger any further, but rather . . . soon [to] be filled with the heavenly food" of the Eucharist. After this ceremony with salt, comes a solemn exorcism in the name of the whole Trinity, calling on Satan to withdraw completely from this person who is about to become God's child.

Here, too, there is a foreshadowing of the significance of water, the principal element to be used in this sacrament. Satan, in this place, is adjured to depart because Christ "is commanding thee . . . He who with sure step walked upon the waters and extended his helping hand to drowning Peter." By this sentence we are reminded that water can be a death dealing as well as a life giving element. This death is now linked up with the possibility of the spiritual death which the evil spirit can inflict. The implication is that since Christ had power over water, which can drown a man, he also has power over Satan who can bring a man to damnation.

The second part of the ceremony is a kind of journey: the admittance of the candidate into the church and a solemn procession to the font. This journey symbolizes the leaving of the devil and his pomps (in the liturgy's vivid phrase), and an entering into the building—the church—to become "stones that live and breathe" (I Pet. 2:5) in that "temple dedicated to the Lord" of which the "chief cornerstone . . . is Jesus Christ himself" (Eph. 2:21).

In proof that he possesses the faith required of such "living stones" the candidate now recites aloud the creed and the Lord's prayer. There is one last injunction to the evil spirit forbidding him to interfere with the candidate's consecration to God. Then the priest imitates the action of Christ who once touched with saliva the senses of the deaf man in the gospel: "And they brought to him a man who was deaf and dumb, with the prayer that he would lay his hand upon him. And he took him aside out of the multitude; he put his fingers into his ears, and spat, and touched his tongue; then he looked up to heaven, and sighed; Ephpheta, he said (that is,

Be opened). Whereupon his ears were opened, and the bond which tied his tongue was loosed, and he talked plainly" (Mark 7:32-35).

This opening of the senses of the candidate prepares him to hear the word of God fruitfully and to say and sing God's praises joyously. Next, touching the person's nostrils, the priest prays by implication that his life may become an "odor of sweetness" before God, and that he may find sweetness in the things of God.

The very first use the person then makes of his newly consecrated power of speech is publicly to renounce Satan and his kingdom. After this comes an anointing which marks the person with Christ's cross once more, and then he makes a solemn profession of faith and loyalty by affirming three times during the recital of the creed, "I do believe." And finally he answers an emphatic "I do" to the question, "Do you wish to be baptized?" This is the second time during the baptism that the creed has been recited. And this profession of faith, as we have seen, is repeated when we offer Mass. It follows that the recitation of the creed should be a real profession of faith, and a renewal of our baptismal vows.

Thirdly, the middle section of the baptismal action is very short, but it contains the essence of the sacrament. It consists in a pouring of water on the head of the candidate and pronouncing at the same time the efficacious words: "I baptize you in the name of the Father and of the Son and of the Holy Ghost."

At this very moment the candidate is cleansed, set free from the power of Satan; his former self is drowned in the waters of baptism, and his newly born Christian self comes out of the waters sharing in the risen life of Christ.

This central action of baptism is a consecration, a transfiguration. In its significance and power it resembles the central section of the Mass. Like the transfigured Christ on Mount Thabor, who shone visibly with the divinity which was in him, the soul of this new member of Christ now shines with a share in that divinity.

The Church herself links the two in the collect for the feast of the Transfiguration, August 6. She says: "O God, who in the glorious transfiguration of thy only-begotten Son didst confirm . . . the truths revealed by faith, and by the voice speaking out of a bright cloud didst miraculously signify the *fulfillment of our adoption as thy children;* in thy mercy deign to make us co-heirs of his kingdom and sharers in his glory."

The symbolism of water is particularly apt for this wonderful rebirth. For one thing, many scientists believe that the first beginnings of life on our planet came from water—up from the sea. In a parallel way, each one's beginning of supernatural life comes about through God's sacramental use of the element of water.

Even the salt we spoke of above strengthens this symbolic meaning, for salt is not only a mineral taken from the earth, but it is also one of the constituents of sea water. And the fluids (all the living matter, in fact) of a man's body resemble sea water. By this very fact the belief that living beings on this earth came first from the sea is given added weight. And what is more to our purpose, we see a new relationship between our two symbolic elements of water and earth (*i.e.*, the mineral from earth, salt). We find, too, a new reference to the fact that baptism is a beginning of life, for this new life begins in water as natural life is also said to have begun in water.

Mysteriously enough, this rebirth is not purely an individual raising to the supernatural life. It is rather the grafting of the new Christian into the living vine (which is Christ), the joining of a new member to the already living mystical body of Christ. By this, the Christian begins to live, not exactly with a new life of his very own, but with a new life which flows to him from the Head, who is Christ. He therefore shares this vitality with all the other Christians who are also members of Christ the Head. This is our divine adoption, and when it occurs we become children of God in a very real sense.

Many references to the fact that man is reborn in baptism are to be found in the liturgy. On Holy Saturday, during the blessing of the font, for example, the Church prays: "O God, even at the beginning of the world thy spirit stirred the water that it might conceive the power of hallowing"—here we see a direct reference to the passage in Genesis which was quoted before: "At the beginning of time . . . darkness hung over the deep; but already over its waters, brooded the Spirit of God" (Gen. 1:1-2).

Then the prayer goes on to mention the flood, and the renewal of life which Noah found after the waters abated and he came out of the ark: "Through water, O God, thou didst wash away the crimes of a guilty world, and prefigure the means of regeneration in the torrent of the flood: for the selfsame substances worked mysteriously *both the death* of vice and the *new beginning* of virtue. . . ." Here are made explicit both meanings of water—water as death, and as life.

Next, dividing the water with his hand in the sign of the cross, the priest brings out clearly the motif of rebirth: "May the Spirit impregnate this water, prepared for the rebirth of men, by the secret inpouring of his divinity, that there may be born from the stainless womb of this divine font a new creation . . . the children of heaven." All through this section of the Holy Saturday liturgy are such references to the lifegiving qualities of water on both natural and supernatural levels. Each reference is more beautiful than the last.

As our Lord said to Nicodemus: "A man cannot see the kingdom of God without being born anew . . . unless birth comes to him from water, and from the Holy Spirit" (John 3:3, 5). Here, too, in the gospel, Christ makes the connection between this water symbol and that of wind: "You must be born anew. The wind breathes where it will, and thou canst hear the sound of it, but knowest nothing of the way it came or the way it goes; so it is, when a man is born by the breath of the Spirit." It sounds as though our Lord were thinking of the wind of Pentecost itself.

The prayers for the blessing of the font are but a paraphrase and an explanation of Christ's own words. This is indeed the living water which he promised to the Samaritan woman at the well.

We should note, also, that when Christ spoke in such mysterious fashion of water, he could expect his hearers to have a vivid awareness of its many-leveled meanings. We have seen water symbols in many stories of Exodus. Two of them are called to mind during the blessing of the font. And with them is united a reference to the rivers of paradise: "He made you flow forth from paradise, commanding you to water all the earth with your four rivers." Here the priest sprinkles some of the water toward the four corners of the earth. And then the prayer goes on: "In the desert he changed your bitterness into a sweet draught, and brought you from the rock to quench his people's thirst."

Again, these people were familiar with the sign of Jonas, and Christ explicitly connects this story of a man remaining in the sea three days and coming back alive, with his own resurrection: "Jonas was three days and three nights in the belly of the sea beast, and the Son of Man will be three days and three nights in the heart of the earth" (Matt. 12:40-41).

Even on the natural level, the people who heard him would be inclined to value the qualities of water. They were men who lived in the open. Weather would enter largely into their calculations. Their out-of-doors, moreover, was mainly desert land. Here water is especially treasured. They would know the difference water can make. Most of them could remember experiences like that which Eliot's old wise man describes—times when they

. . . . came down to a temperate valley,
Wet, below the snow line, smelling of vegetation,
With a running stream and a water-mill beating the
   darkness . . .[50]

Theirs was a vivid sense of the refreshment of water because they had made journeys through hot dry land on foot, and then had come slowly into fertile valleys, feeling gradually the welcome dampness of shade by a stream with trees along its banks. It is no wonder that the imagery of still waters threads through the psalms. They are full of such pictures as that of Psalm 22: "He gives me a resting place where there is pasture, and leads me out by cool waters, to make me live anew" (Ps. 22:2).

The fourth section of the baptismal ceremony is a bestowing of gifts, and here can be seen an analogy with the fourth section of the Mass wherein we receive the great gift of Christ himself. The gifts given here are three: a special anointing with fragrant chrism (like a gift of perfume), a white garment, and a lighted candle.

Chrism's fragrance is related to the element of air, for it permeates the atmosphere and is carried upon its currents. By baptism, as the rite says explicitly, the soul becomes a temple of God, filled with the fragrance of God's presence, and perfumed like a temple with the incense of worship.

The baptismal anointing, with oil which comes to us as a part of earth's fruitfulness, bestows a share in the royal priesthood of Christ. As the Mass preface for the Kingship of our Lord Jesus Christ says so well, God "anointed his only begotten Son . . . with the oil of gladness to be a priest forever and king of the whole world." And it is to this living Christ who is everlastingly priested that we are united at baptism. Through this anointing the new Christian is qualified and given a responsibility to take some part in Christ's priestly work of worshipping God and saving souls.

The white garment symbolizes the perfect cleansing which

the baptismal waters have effected: "Receive this white garment, and see that you wear it without stain to the judgment seat of our Lord Jesus Christ, that you may enjoy life everlasting." This is the robe the Christian will wear when he stands in that city whose "twelve gates [are] twelve single pearls, one pearl for each gate [—the city whose] temple is the Lord God Almighty . . . the Lamb [the city which has no], need of sun or moon [for] the glory of God shines there, and the Lamb gives it light" (Apoc. 21:21 ff.).

Then standing "before the throne in the Lamb's presence, clothed in white robes" (Apoc. 7:9), they will cry out: "To our God, who sits on the throne, and to the Lamb, all saving power belongs" (Apoc. 8:10). This is the culmination of that movement toward salvation and the promised land of glory, which began in Exodus with the blood of the paschal lamb.

Like the final section of the Mass, the fifth section of the baptismal ceremony is a kind of *"Ite, missa est,"* an injunction to go into the journey of life and fulfill a mission. The priest says, "Go in peace, and may the Lord be with you." It is as if he were saying: Go out now, wearing the baptismal robe, carrying the candle of faith, and fulfill your function of being a sweet fragrance of praise before God and man. This farewell reminds us of the many such wayfaring wishes found in the Mass: "The Lord be with you—Go with God."

2. *The Eucharist:* "This is my Body. This is the chalice of my Blood—A mystery of faith."

After our cleansing and new birth through the waters of baptism, we need nourishment, and so we are fed with the sacred Bread and Wine of the Eucharist. We are now "children new born, and all [our] craving must be for the soul's pure milk, that will nurture [us] into salvation, once [we] have tasted, as [we] have surely tasted, the goodness of the Lord" (I Pet. 2:2).

Man needs food for his body. But also, as we have seen earlier, he needs nourishment for mind and heart from social sharing with his fellow man. We receive the Eucharist, therefore, in a social situation—a banquet where Christ the head of the family invites us to come to the table of peace and unity with him and the other members of his household.

We as individuals are nourished spiritually by this divine Food. But more than this, the whole body of Christ is fed when we receive Holy Communion. When one part is nourished, does not the whole body profit? And so, since we are members of one another, the Food which strengthens and refreshes each individual also strengthens and refreshes the whole mystical body of Christ.

In this connection the familiar symbol of a journey has relevance. We know that for many years two important and meaningful journeys, or processions up to the altar of God, took place within the very structure of the Mass itself. The first was a carrying of gifts to the altar—often they were the bread and wine for the sacrifice itself. This was the offertory procession. It is now seldom carried out, mainly for practical reasons. But the ushers who carry the collection baskets journey in our stead, and our part is to let them take our gifts and present them to the Lord.

The connection, however, should not be forgotten. If we thought more often about the fact that our contribution made during the offertory has special relevance to the great sacrifice itself, we should present our gifts in a particularly joyous spirit. These material things, moreover, symbolize the gift we are making of ourselves and all that concerns us. These are the presents we offer to God, and he in his turn, not wishing to be outdone by us, will invite us to his table and give us the overwhelming gift of his divine Son as our spiritual sustenance.

God gives us this gift in the fourth section of the Mass, the communion, where there is another journey, another procession, balancing the offertory procession. This time we go up, not to give a gift to God, but to receive one from him. Because this is a solemn procession, made in togetherness with our fellow Christians, the Church encourages us to sing while we walk to and from the communion rail, for she is well aware that singing both strengthens and expresses our unity.

The Eucharist, then, is the food which unifies the whole mystical body of Christ. We are a part of this great reality, and so our communion, which is indeed a visit with Christ present in our individual soul, is also much more. Hence to gain its great graces we should be conscious of its multiple effects and significances. A postcommunion for the first Friday in Lent sums up these thoughts: "Pour into our hearts, O Lord, the Spirit of thy love, so that we who have eaten our fill of one and the same heavenly bread may . . . come to be of one mind." Nourishment, refreshment, unity—these are the fruits of the Eucharistic banquet.

We might summarize the things we have been saying by focusing our attention for a moment on the two main symbols connected with the Holy Eucharist, considered in its sacramental aspects. These symbols are those of food and the journey. Food means much in the way of union, peace, concord, hospitality, as well as nourishment; the journeys are processions to and from the altar of God to give him our gifts and to receive his gift in return. Just as we cannot have a one-man banquet, neither can we have an one-man procession. Both are social activities, uniting us with Christ and with each other. Of these two, the absolutely essential symbol and reality, is that of food—bread and wine. But the processions are meaningful and help us to a better understanding of this great sacrament.

Much more might be said of the Eucharist, but since we have discussed some of its aspects in connection with the first circle, the Mass—of which it is an integral part—we will not say more here, but will turn to the sacrament through which we come to Christian maturity.

3. *Confirmation:* "May the Holy Spirit come upon you . . ."

The sacrament through which we reach spiritual maturity and independence is that of confirmation. Its reception makes us adult Christians, able to bear responsibility for others and to contribute our services to the Christian community.

One way of analyzing the ceremony is to see it as structured around two interrelated actions. The first is an extending of the bishop's hands over the candidates. Here he calls into play all the fullness of his power to invoke the Holy Spirit with his gifts: "The Spirit of wisdom and of understanding. Amen. The Spirit of counsel and fortitude. Amen. The Spirit of knowledge and piety. Amen. Fill them with the Spirit of thy fear, and seal them with the sign of the Cross of Christ unto life everlasting."

The second is an anointing with chrism, the fragrant mixture of oil and balsam (symbols related to the fruitfulness of earth, and to fragrance carried on air). Along with this anointing comes the giving of a new name to each candidate and a slight blow on the cheek. Various meanings are attached to this last gesture. It symbolizes the kiss of peace given in former times during the reception of the sacrament. And it is also taken in our times as symbolizing the fortitude with which the newly confirmed person is endowed through the Holy Spirit.

This is something like the significance of the blow on the shoulder given at the conferring of knighthood, when the words "I dub thee knight" are spoken. In a similar way, a confirmed Christian is a knight of Christ, expected to show courage in daily living, and even heroic fortitude in times of special danger and suffering. Because, moreover, he is now invested with new responsibilities, he also receives a new name which puts him under the protection of a specially chosen saint.

Four symbols, especially relevant to the Holy Spirit, can be found in this ceremony: the oil for anointing, a dwelling place, and implicit in the reference to the Holy Spirit, the symbols of fire and wind.

As to the first, the oil—the Holy Spirit is often referred to as being himself an unction, an anointing. We see this in the hymn *"Veni Creator Spiritus*—Come Creator Spirit" where he is called the "soul's anointing from above." Anointing is a comforting and healing action. In Psalm 22, for example, we read: "Richly thou dost anoint my head with oil. . . . All my life thy goodness pursues me" (22:5-6). And the Holy Spirit is frequently named the Comforter.

Furthermore, for many years it was believed that oil actually penetrated the skin and strengthened the muscles, and here we can see the relationship between this idea and the fortitude which is one of the gifts of confirmation. As oil makes bodies agile and supple to escape opponents in a wrestling match, so the anointing at confirmation helps us in our wrestling with the powers of darkness. Such suppleness and strength are needed because "It is not against flesh and blood that we enter the lists; we have to do with princedoms and powers, with those who have mastery of the world in these dark days" (Eph. 6:12).

Again, during the conferring of the sacrament, we find clear mention of the second symbol, a dwelling place of God, a temple of his glory. The prayer is: May the Holy Spirit "graciously consecrate their hearts as a temple of his glory by dwelling within them." A new depth of meaning can be found when we connect these words with the opening words of the ceremony: "May the Holy Ghost come upon you and may the power of the most High keep you from sin."

If we eliminate for the moment the last four words in this

quotation, we find that the sentence comes directly from St. Luke's account of the incarnation of Christ: "The Holy Spirit will come upon thee, and the power of the most High will over-shadow thee" (Luke 1:35). Then Luke goes on immediately to say that therefore the holy One who shall be born of Mary shall be the Son of God.

By these words Mary became the living temple of God, who at this moment was made incarnate in her. In an analogous fashion, we are made temples of God at confirmation. Moreover, as Cardinal Suhard has said in *Growth or Decline,* "Christ must become incarnate in each generation." Now this expresses very well the purpose of confirmation which is not only to make us dwelling places of the Spirit of God, but to form us as apostles, who in his strength will go out and work so that Christ may become incarnate in our own generation.

This means that like St. Paul we are to be "in travail until [we] can see Christ's image formed" in our fellow men (Gal. 4:19). We are to help toward the "completion of him who everywhere and in all things is complete" (Eph. 1:23). Then when we have spent ourselves in order to make Christ incarnate once again, the Father, looking on us and on our associates may see his Son living out his life anew in our own country, and city, and home—in our own twentieth century.

Confirmation, moreover, being especially the sacrament of the Holy Spirit, we speak of it as a new Pentecost. This idea of a renewal of the happenings of Pentecost calls to our minds the first coming of the Holy Spirit in fire and wind.

Fire means love and wrath; it means guidance by light. Wind means breath and words—it can be a whirlwind coming in power, or a cool breeze. Several of these meanings coalesce during the events of the first Pentecost. We know that the great wind came announcing the Spirit. He appeared under the form of tongues of fire—a fire which transforms the two spiritual powers of man, his intellect and his will. Man's intellect is transfigured by the light of the Spirit, and his will is warmed and set aflame by the Spirit of love.

It is especially fitting that the flames which appear should have been in the form of tongues. Tongues, for one thing, cooperate with breath to form words. These words, shaped by the wind and flame of the Spirit, are to go out and set the world aflame with God's truth and love.

The gift of tongues also becomes a sign and instrument of unity here at Pentecost. We have learned that it was through the breaking up of the unified language of the human race at Babel that the original solidarity of mankind was disrupted (Genesis 11). Now at Pentecost there is a welding anew of the nations which were broken up in the beginning of days. In those times, men refused to love God, and preferred to defy him. God therefore caused men to speak diverse languages. In this way the unity of the race was broken.

But at Pentecost, by the gift of tongues—an appearance of tongues of flame, and also a power given to the apostles to speak in their own tongue while being understood in many languages—men were endowed with zeal and ability to go on apostolic mission with intent to unify all things in Christ. They were to help in making all one, as Christ and the Father are one. And all this unity is personified in the Spirit of Love —the Spirit who appeared in the wind and fire of Pentecost.

This wind of the Spirit is also a sweet fragrance of worship. This is a symbolism inherent in the fragrance of chrism used for the anointing. Like the old Isaac, when he was about to bless his son Jacob, God our Father can now say: "How it breathes about this son of mine, the fragrance of earth when the Lord's blessing is on it!" (Gen. 27:27). And this fragrance is to be carried out from us on the wind of our words as a perfume drawing souls to God. When this happens we are truly fruitful Christians, and God gives us "dew from heaven and fruitful soil, corn and wine in plenty" (Gen. 27:28).

During this discussion of confirmation, we have considered it as the sacrament of Christian maturity, and have seen some of the fruits which are a result of its reception. Now with our maturation and assuming of responsibility towards God and our fellow man, comes also the possibility of giving offense. The next sacrament to be discussed treats of the means of making reparation when offense has been given.

4. *Penance:* "Go in peace, thy sins are forgiven."

With our arrival at maturity, as we have said, we not only have new powers, but also new responsibilities. With further responsibility comes further possibility of failure. This means that since we are adults we are bound to accept the consequences of our actions.

If, for example, we commit a felony, the state has a right to call us to judgment and to impose a penalty. It means, on a more familiar level, that if we have offended one to whom we owe honor or love, we express our sorrow and make some kind of reparation. Then the person offended judges whether our reparation makes us worthy of forgiveness.

On the supernatural level, sorrow for evil doing, judgment, and reparation are the three divisions of the sacrament of penance. These three actions are basic to its structure: 1) the voluntary appearance of the sinner before the tribunal of God's justice in the confessional, and his demonstration of sorrow by recounting his sins; 2) the judgment arrived at by God's representative, the priest, as to the sincerity of the penitent's sorrow, and following upon his decision, the forgiveness of sin which comes through the absolution spoken in God's name; 3) the instructing of the penitent to make reparation by saying some specific prayers or doing some good deed.

Images of the priest as a judge presiding and making a decision, and the gesture of absolution made in the sign of the cross are the symbols used here. The cross, of course, signifies our saving by the blood which Christ shed for us: "This is my blood, of the new testament," he says, "shed for many unto the remission of sins" (Matt. 26:28).

The cross is the sign of our redemption from the kingdom of Satan. By this cross we were saved once for all, but in another sense, we are newly saved every time its effects are applied to our individual souls in their special situations. As the prophet says, "By his bruises we were healed" (Isaias 53:5). This cross is the tree of continually renewed life. The Good Friday hymn, *Crux Fidelis,* addresses the cross in these beautiful words which point up the symbol of the tree:

> Faithful Cross, of trees created,
>   Noblest tree of all art thou;
> Forest none bears trees as thou art,
>   Like in leaf or flower or bough.
> Dear the nails and dear the timber;
>   Dear the load they bear aloft.

The cross of absolution is meant to remind us of the tree of Calvary's cross. And also because it takes away our sins, the sacrament of penance is related to the cleansing powers of baptism. Then too, it is a kind of healing, since the forgiveness of sins brings peace to the soul, and with peace come health and well being. The relationship between forgiveness and health is brought into focus at least twice in the gospels: first in the instance of the paralyzed man whose friends lowered him through the skylight, and then in the scene where Christ heals the beggar at the pool of Bethsaida.

The first happened one day when people were crowding around our Lord. Some men tried to bring an invalid in so that he might be cured. But they could not get through the crowd. Then some one of them had an idea. They carried the sick man up on the roof and let him down with ropes tied to his pallet until he rested at Christ's feet. But to the surprise of the bystanders, our Lord said: "Son, take courage, thy sins are forgiven" (Matt. 9:2).

Probably the man was filled with relieved joy. Perhaps he did not care if he were ever healed so long as this greater gift of interior peace was his. But his friends must have been disappointed. After all their hard work, and their ingenuity in reaching the Master, he did not seem to understand why they had taken all this trouble.

Then some others in the crowd, men of more learning than the rest, began to mutter, "He is talking blasphemously" (Matt. 9:3). By this speech they showed that they realized Christ was here claiming to be God—for only God can forgive offenses done to himself.

In answer, Christ says that he will prove his power to forgive sins (and by this, of course, he also proves his divinity): "Tell me," he said, "which command is more lightly given, to say to a man, Thy sins are forgiven, or to say, Rise up and walk? And now to convince you that the Son of Man has authority to forgive sins . . . (here he spoke to the palsied man), Rise up, take thy bed with thee, and go home. And he rose up, and went back to his house" (Matt. 9:5-7).

The second example in which forgiveness and healing are juxtaposed is the cure of the man at the pool of Bethsaida (John 5). The man had been ill for thirty-eight years—longer than Christ had been living on earth. As the gospel says, "Jesus saw him lying there, and knew that he had waited a long time" (John 5:6).

Our Lord asked him if he wished to recover his strength, but the poor man, much as we do, had it all planned. There was only one way, he thought, that he could be healed. If someone would come along and help him just at the right time he might get down to the waters first after they had been stirred by the angel, for the power of the waters was there only in the moments immediately after the angel had disturbed them.

But "Jesus said to him, Rise up . . . and walk." And he was healed. Moreover, as we find out a little later, his sins were also forgiven at this same time. The gospel does not tell us that the man knew, at the time of his cure, that he had received this spiritual healing.

It merely relates an incident which happened a little later: "But afterwards when Jesus found him [he] said to him, Behold, thou hast recovered thy strength; do not sin any more, for fear that worse should befall thee" (John 5:14). By this command, our Lord makes it clear that he had not only healed the man's paralyzed body, but also restored his soul by a forgiveness of sins.

Now when a responsible Christian, conscious of his sins, seeks to make reparation to God, he is enabled to do this by means of the sacrament of penance. Here he, like the two paralyzed men of the gospel, finds forgiveness and healing. This is, therefore, one of the sacraments needed by the mature Christian.

But maturity brings not only power to sin but other powers which function for the good of the individual and of society. With one of these powers, and the sacrament which consecrates it, we shall next be concerned. This is the power given to man and woman of cooperating with God in bringing new human beings into the world.

5. *Matrimony:* "With this ring I thee wed."

The mature person should be capable of parenthood. It is normal for him to rejoice when he sees his individual life united with another's and their conjoined lives shared by children which are their own. A man may use this power to become a co-creator with God, or he may consecrate it to God in virginity, in order to free himself for a larger and wider love. This love will be centered more singly on Christ, and yet at the same time it will radiate out from this union with

Christ to bring the good things of God to all his human children. Parenthood, then, can be of the physical or the spiritual order.

The natural power to transmit life is consecrated in the sacrament of matrimony. We have seen, just above, that penance is structured like a judgment rendered in a court of law. Similarly, matrimony is like another human and social deed, namely, the making of a contract.

This contract is entered into when both bride and groom pledge their loyalty to each other in the presence of God's representative, the priest. Unlike the other sacraments which are primarily administered by the priest or bishop, this sacrament is administered by the bride and groom to each other, with the priest functioning as a necessary witness. There are three parts to the actual ceremony: 1) a conversation and a promise; 2) the blessing and giving of the ring; 3) the prayers for the stability of this holy city of God—the new home.

The first part of the ceremony is, then, a questioning and a consent, followed by a promise of fidelity: "I, John, take thee, Mary, for my lawful wife, to have and to hold from this day forward, for better, for worse, for richer, for poorer, in sickness and in health, till death do us part." This same promise is then made by the bride. Then the priest pronounces over them the words: "I unite you in marriage, in the name of the Father and of the Son and of the Holy Ghost. Amen."

After this he sprinkles them with holy water. Blessings in water always remind us of our baptismal life—our risen life in Christ. It is because we are baptized Christians that this natural contract becomes a sacrament—something above and beyond the purely natural goodness of human marriage in itself.

Because we are baptized, the water of human love is changed at a wedding feast into the rich wine of supernatural love. Such wine, properly cared for, grows mellower with time, so that like the steward at Cana's wedding feast, the Christian man and wife can also say after long years together: The best wine has been kept until now (John 2:10).

In the second section of the ceremony comes the blessing and giving of the ring. Frequently today, there are two rings, one for the bride and one for the groom. The ring is a symbol of continuity and unbroken wholeness, and at the same time, by its relationship to all circular movement, it symbolizes the change and progress of days and events. These days and events will make the couple's life together a varied one. Yet no joy or sorrow should have power to break the perfect circle of their love consecrated here in God's sacramental presence. Their promise is expressed simply and beautifully: "With this ring I thee wed, and promise to thee my fidelity."

At the last, there are a few prayers which refer to their life together as God's holy temple, his city of Jerusalem—that Jerusalem which appears "like a bride who has adorned herself to meet her husband" (Apoc. 21:2). And the priest prays that the Lord may be to them a tower of strength protecting the city.

During the Marriage Mass which follows the actual wedding, a special nuptial blessing is given in two parts—one after the *Pater Noster,* and the other just before the final blessing of the Mass itself. These blessings have a natural psychological value as well as a purely supernatural one, because they hold up for admiration and imitation the valiant women of the Old Testament who were good wives.

The bride, especially, is advised in the first prayer to be "dear to her husband as Rachel was; wise as Rebecca; long-lived and faithful as Sara." This placing of the new home life in the stream of a rich tradition, and this presenting of examples of others who have succeeded in the same undertaking, encourages the newly married couple to found their home on similar strong foundations.

This blessing is concluded after the postcommunion

prayer. And here again we are in company with the great people of the Old Testament: "May the God of Abraham, the God of Isaac, the God of Jacob be with you, and may he bless you greatly in every way . . ."

The fact that the Church is most anxious for her children to understand and treasure these blessings, is clearly proved by recent legislation allowing more use of the English language in the ceremony. Even the blessings which occur during the Mass itself may now be given in the vernacular. But whether they are said in English or in Latin, we are able to read them in our own language, and to ponder them thoughtfully. Such meditation will repay in many ways those married or about to be married.

Such Christian marriages are a source of grace to those making the holy contract and to the whole mystical body of Christ. They function, moreover, to bring into the world new human beings who are also capable of becoming members of Christ's body which is the Church. The next sacrament we will discuss is, accordingly, that which invests man with power to bring the children of such marriages into this new life—this real sharing in God's own kind of life.

6. *Holy Orders:* ". . . to offer sacrifice, to bless, to govern, to preach, and to baptize."

Of all the ceremonies surrounding the sacraments, the most elaborate are those belonging to holy orders. As in baptism and the Mass, we find here, too, a five-fold structure: 1) a journey; 2) a conversation; 3) the prayer like a Mass preface, imposition of hands, and anointing—this central section contains the essence of the sacrament; 4) an immediate actualizing of the new priestly powers by the con-celebration of the Mass; 5) a preparation for a journey. Like baptism and the Mass, this sacrament also has two preparatory sections, an important central section, and two concluding parts.

There is, furthermore, a profusion—almost a welter—of symbolism: ships and water, medicine and fragrance, fire and dwellings, journeys and oil, clothing and a family life lived with God. We cannot discuss all of these in detail, but will refer to the symbols now and then while outlining the structure.

In the first section we find an invitation: "Let those who are to be ordained to the Order of priesthood come forward." Then comes a short but highly meaningful journey, for here the roll of candidates is called, and each one takes a step forward. This signifies the deliberate intention to walk into a new state, to take on the privileges and responsibilities of the priesthood.

Then in the second section the bishop asks the people if they are aware of any reason that these candidates should be refused ordination. These men are to be "other Christs"; they are, as the bishop here says, to guide the ship on which the people will come to God. And "since . . . the master of a ship and the passengers have common motives for security or fear," they should agree in opinion as to the fitness of the candidates for ordination.

Immediately there follows an instruction on the duties and privileges of the priesthood: "Let your doctrine be spiritual medicine for the people of God; let the odor of your life be the delight of the Church of Christ; so that by your example you may build up the house, that is the family of God. . . ."

Here are indirect and symbolic references to all the sacraments which the priest will have power to administer. We find the *medicine* of penance and extreme unction, the *fragrance* of baptismal and other anointings; and the *building* of the *house* and *family* of God through: 1) the consecration of matrimony; 2) baptism, which adds new human beings as living stones to God's house, and as new-born members of God's family; 3) the Eucharist, which sustains and increases the life of the family.

Then with the invocation of all the family of God in the Litany of the Saints, the third section begins. When the litany is finished, the candidates come forward and the bishop, in silence, lays both hands on the head of each one; after this, all the priests who are present also perform the same action in silence. This is a most impressive moment. By this gesture the power of the Holy Spirit is called down, and the candidates are invested with priestly powers.

Next comes a prayer like a Mass preface: "It is truly meet and just, right and available to salvation that we should give thanks to thee, O Holy Lord . . . Who dost continually increase and perfect the growth of our rational nature in a most orderly and suitable manner. Hence also have grown up the degrees of priesthood and the office of levites instituted by *mystic symbols."* Then the bishop goes on to recall the priests of the Old Testament who offered "saving sacrifices." And he asks: "Bestow, then . . . the dignity of the Priesthood upon these thy servants; renew in them the spirit of holiness. . . . May the spirit of all justice shine forth in them. . . ."

By this prayer, as well as on other occasions in the rite, these young men, like those Christians we have seen receiving the sacrament of matrimony, are placed in the stream of a great tradition and shown the dignity of their calling.

Now they are invested with the priestly stole (the "yoke of the Lord; [whose] yoke is sweet and his burden light"), and they are given the chasuble which signifies charity. It may be that this symbolism has become attached to this garment because it envelops the whole person in its folds, and charity "believes all things, hopes all things, endures all things."

During this third section also, the bishop invokes the Holy Spirit and anoints the hands of the candidates with the sign of the cross; then he covers the whole palm of each one's hands with consecrating oil. While doing this he prays that the Lord will consecrate and sanctify these hands, "That whatsoever they shall bless may be blessed, and whatsoever they shall consecrate shall be consecrated and sanctified."

The two consecrated hands of each new priest are then lightly bound together with strips of linen, and each one is presented with a chalice containing wine and water, and a paten with a host. Meanwhile the bishop says, "Receive power to offer sacrifice to God and to celebrate Mass, as well for the living as for the dead, in the name of the Lord." The newly ordained priests now wash their hands, and then each one presents a lighted candle to the bishop and kisses his pastoral ring in token of fealty.

Next, in the fourth section, these new priests exercise their sacrificial powers for the first time by offering Mass along with the presiding bishop. They begin with the offertory and say all the prayers in unison. At this time they actually co-consecrate along with the bishop, and offer Christ to the Father at the same time that he does.

The last part of the ordination, the fifth section, takes place after the Mass prayer of thanksgiving for Holy Communion ("May thy body, O Lord, which I have received . . ."). It is a preparation for the priest's going out into the world to win men for Christ. In this way it is also a sending forth on a journey, like the fifth part of the Mass and of baptism. When we come to the last anointing we shall see another, similar injunction.

For this part of the ceremony, Mass is interrupted. Here the bishop repeats the words of Christ: "I will not now call you servants, but my friends, because you have known all the things which I have wrought in the midst of you. Alleluia. You are my friends, if you do the things that I command you. Receive in you the Holy Ghost, the Paraclete."

Then the newly ordained priests make profession of the faith they will preach. To do this they recite the creed. After this the bishop gives them power to forgive sins. He imposes his hands on the head of each one and says: "Receive the Holy Ghost; whose sins thou shalt forgive they are forgiven them; and whose sins thou shalt retain they are retained."

He next unfolds the chasubles which have lain folded on their shoulders, praying: "May the Lord clothe thee with the stole of innocence." And after he has asked, "Dost thou promise to me and my successors reverence and obedience?" he receives the answer, "I promise." Then he takes each one's folded hands in his own hands and gives each new priest the kiss of peace, praying that the peace of the Lord may be always with him.

Reminding them once again of the holy seriousness of their vocation, he blesses them "in the order of priesthood . . . that [they] may offer, for the sins . . . of the people, sacrifice of propitiation to Almighty God."

The Mass is now resumed and continues up to the final blessing, after which those who have been ordained are instructed that, following their first Mass, they are to say "three other Masses: one of the Holy Ghost, another of the Blessed Mary ever Virgin, and a third for the faithful departed," and, adds the bishop, "Pray to Almighty God for me also." Now the last gospel is said, and the ceremony of ordination has come to an end.

All of these six great sacraments have one final end in view: the soul's coming at last to its home with God and its everlasting joy and fulfillment found in the beatific vision. The seventh sacrament is the last anointing, extreme unction. One of the reasons for its name is the fact that this anointing normally takes place last; that is, after the Christian has been anointed in baptism, in confirmation, and in holy orders (if he is a priest).

This sacrament shows by the words used in its administration that it is an instrument of healing for body as well as soul. The healing is to enable the sick person to take up his normal life once more if it be God's will. And the emphasis in the prayers is placed on this kind of health. If, however, the time has come for the Christian to reach his final goal, the last anointing finishes the preparation for glory which was begun with baptism, and continued through life.

7. *The Last Anointing:* "Graciously bless him with perfect health within and without."

The full flowering of the grace first given at baptism and subsequently increased throughout the Christian life comes with the step across the threshold of death into the vision of God. At this moment our destiny is sealed. It will never be changed. This is true not only of the destination of the soul for hell or heaven, but even of the capacity of the soul for happiness. The soul is, as it were, "frozen" in whatever state it is in at the moment of death. Its capacity for God can never again increase.

Since this is so, two things become very important: our daily and hourly receptivity to the divine life and its growth in us, and the dispositions in which we shall be when we step across death into life. For the first, the six sacraments we have been discussing earlier are most wonderful helps. For the second, the sacrament especially provided is extreme unction—the anointing unto glory.

When we consider only the ceremonies properly belonging to the sacrament itself, we find that it is structured in four sections. But as we shall see later, a possible fifth section corresponding to the last sections of Mass, baptism, and holy orders, may be seen if we include the prayers said for one in the final agony of death.

The proper parts are: 1) the symbol of the priest's entrance into the house where the sick person is, and his invoking of blessings upon it; 2) the cleansing through the confiteor and the prayer against the powers of the devil, followed by an invocation of the saints; 3) the anointing of the senses—this is the essential part of the sacrament; 4) the concluding prayers.

If, however, we include in the pattern the beautiful prayers for the departing soul, beginning, "Go forth, O Christian soul . . ." we have a five part structure, with the central section containing the essence of the sacrament. This fifth part is, however, not properly included in the sacrament itself.

Besides the structure, two things are very noticeable about this sacrament. The first is that that all the prayers and blessings have to do with health and healing, joy and return to daily life. The second is that special provision, extraneous to the sacrament, is made for the person whose time to die has actually come.

During the priest's entrance into the house we hear: "May there enter this house . . . unending happiness, heaven-sent prosperity, joy undisturbed, practical kindness, and unfailing health." May God "deliver them from all harm in this their dwelling place."

In the second part, the confiteor is said to aid the sick person to repent for his sins. Then the priest does two things: he prays that "all the power of the devil against [him] may be at an end," and that the mother of God and all the saints and angels may use their power to protect him.

Not only is Satan to be gone, but his place is to be filled by the friends of God, so that the soul may not be like the person described by Christ in St. Matthew's gospel (12:43-45). This sinner was freed from the evil spirit, but no other good being came to fill up the space.

Therefore when the devil came back looking for a home, he found that soul, "empty, and swept out, and neatly set in order." And so "with seven other spirits, more wicked" than himself, he returned and dwelt there. This anointed Christian, on the other hand, will have no space left for the evil one, since his soul will be protected by the presence of the whole court of heaven which has been invited to come and dwell with him.

During the anointing of eyes, ears, nostrils, mouth, hands, feet, which is the third and essential part of the sacrament, the priest prays that the sick person may be mercifully forgiven by God: "Through this holy Unction and His most tender mercy, may the Lord forgive thee whatever sin thou hast committed by the sense of sight (or hearing, smell, taste or speech, touch or motion)."

In the fourth part, the prayers ask only that the Lord may be a "tower of strength." There is almost an insistence that health be restored: "Cure the ailments of this thy sick servant; heal his wounds; forgive his sins; relieve him of all miseries of body and mind." The prayer even asks that "being made well again . . . he may be able to take up anew the duties of his state in life." And at last we hear, "Do thou lift him up and restore him to Thy holy Church with every advantage that could be wished for." This is the note upon which the sacramental rite ends.

However, if the soul is actually entering upon its last struggle before death, there are majestic prayers said in order to help in his mysterious journey to God. Some of the phrases are true poetry: "Go forth from this world, O Christian soul, in the name of God the Father almighty, who created you; in the name of Jesus Christ, Son of the living God, who suffered for you; in the name of the Holy Ghost who was poured forth upon you." Then the saints and the nine choirs of angels are called upon to be with him, and the prayer pleads: "May your dwelling be in peace this day, and may your abode be in holy Sion."

"O merciful God," the priest continues, "bind this redeemed member to the united body of the Church . . . admit him to the mystery of thy reconciliation." "I entrust you to Him whose creature you are; that . . . you may return to your Maker who formed you out of the slime of the earth. May the glorious choirs of angels meet your soul as it leaves the body. . . . May the face of Jesus Christ appear to you mild and joyful. . . . Let God arise and let his enemies be scattered. . . . As smoke vanishes, so let them vanish away; as wax melteth before the fire. . . . But the just shall feast and rejoice before the face of God."

In these lines are earth, of which man was formed, air in the vanishing of the smoke, fire in which the wax of enmity is to melt. After this, the priest prays: "May Christ, the Son of the living God, place you in the green pastures of his paradise, and may He the true shepherd, acknowledge you as one of His own sheep . . . may you enjoy the sweetness of the divine vision for all eternity. Amen." Thereafter, with a wealth of imagery and allusion to the Old Testament and the New, we hear about many who were delivered by the Lord: Noah from the flood, the youths from the fiery furnace, Daniel from the lions' den, and many others. By these examples, God is made mindful of the mercies he has shown to others, and implored to show the same mercy to this dying Christian.

With such riches does God endow those whom he has invited to become members of his body the Church. A lifetime could be spent in meditating on the significance and power inherent in the structure and symbols of the sacraments. It is, however, time for us to think about the third circle, that of the consecration of the day hours by the office.

CHAPTER EIGHT

Of the Office: Third Circle

> The ultimate basis of the excellence
> of the Divine Office is the canticle
> of the Word in the bosom of the Divinity
> and in creation.
> The Word is the Canticle that God
> inwardly sings to Himself.
>
> We then prayed the psalms in Christ,
> as He now prays them in us . . .
>
> MARMION [51]

A CIRCLE of petition and praise, of adoration, admiration, and gratitude wheels around the Mass and the life-cycle of the sacraments. This third one is a day-circle because its movement is based on the cycle of the sun's rising and waning light.

Both stability and change are apparent in this basic pattern since the kaleidoscopic days round into weeks, and returning Sundays ring out their "Glory be to the Father, and to the Son, and to the Holy Spirit" at each new beginning.

Furthermore, a satisfying ceremony and majesty are here—a majesty like the grave marching of planets—for the pattern is also shaped by the great turning circle of the yearly seasons. This majestic pattern of prayer is the office.

1. The office: what it is, what it can mean to us

What, precisely, is the office? It is the official daily praise which the Church, the mystical body of Christ, offers to God—a praise composed principally of God's own words as found in the scriptures. It is made up of eight sections called *Hours*, one Hour for each three hours of the day. Each Hour's theme and symbols are set by the occupations natural to the different times of day.

This official prayer presents, as we shall see, very real and practical opportunities to every Christian—opportunities within our reach from the very fact that we are Christians, sharing in the acts of Christ and the doings of the other members of his mystical body. Exploring the office and living with an awareness of the symbolism which is its gift to our every day can be an adventure. In this adventure we discover that every day in the office (in Dylan Thomas' words already quoted) the "whole world sings its morning of praise."

The office is a most useful instrument for adding fresh effectiveness to our private and communal prayer, a new dimension to our offering of the Mass, and a newly awakened delight in the whole round earth.

Suppose that we could have a form of prayer which would include all our moods of joy and wrath, of serenity and sorrow—every terror of storm and earthquake, all fields warm under sun, or crags looming over the ocean. Suppose further that this prayer were to be expressed in the most sublime poetry, the poetry of the psalms which has been warmed in the hearts and on the tongues of people for thousands of years.

Even more wonderfully, suppose that this worship contained the favorite prayers of the Word of God, the Wisdom of God, who is Christ—the very prayers he prayed and quoted during his days on earth.

At the Last Supper, for example, because it was a paschal

supper, he must have recited the psalms called *Hallel* (113-118). And these are now said at the Hour of Vespers, the Hour which consecrates early evening, supper time. We know, too, that he quoted Psalm 21 on the cross when he said, "My God, my God, why hast thou forsaken me." This psalm, and all the other 149 psalms, are said in the office at different times. And as Dom Marmion says of these prayers when we pray them in the office: "We then prayed them in him, as he now prays them in us." Knowing all these things, would we not feel privileged if this kind of prayer were given us by God?

We are aware that priests and certain religious orders pray the office, but does it belong to everybody? Can people in our hasty modern world share in it? They can—and this in four eminently practical ways.

First of all, we can be conscious of this great stream of adoration and praise which hourly flows to God from that body of Christ to which we belong. We can deliberately unite ourselves to this worship. This can be done by a swift turning of the heart to God, a silent consent to all the glory given him by those whose duty it is to pray the office.

Secondly, we can learn about the symbolism of the different sections of the office, and in this way we will find the hours of our days taking on a new grace and meaning. To help us acquire this wisdom is the primary purpose of this chapter.

Thirdly, we may choose psalms or hymns from the Bible, missal, or breviary (which is the book of the office) suitable for different parts of the day and insert them among our measures of time to consecrate the hours and lift our minds to heaven.

If, in the fourth place, we are not bound to the recitation of the office, we may nevertheless freely choose to pray some selected portions of it when time permits. This is being done increasingly by individuals and in homes. For this purpose many shortened forms of the divine office are available. Again, most of us have had at least some little experience with the short office of the Sodality or the Little Office of the Blessed Virgin Mary. Both of these are structured, like the Hours of the breviary, to follow the rising and waning of light. And the latter is a real part of the divine office itself. The *Short Breviary* (Collegeville, Minn.) is a rich mine of thoughts for meditation and selections for recitation, while the divine office itself is also available in English.

In writing this explanation of the office, however, our purpose is not particularly to persuade people to begin the recitation of the office, but rather, by pointing out the beauty of its structure and symbolism, to help Christians to find a new wisdom, a new delight in their heritage. Thinking about these things can help those bound to the recitation of the office to a deeper appreciation of their privilege; it can possibly arouse some others to share the stream of praise in one of the four ways described above, or it can serve simply to supply us with some new knowledge about Christianity and the world in which Christianity functions.

The office is, first of all, a prayer having (like the Mass) a certain unchanging framework, called the *ordinary*. This gives it stability and strengthens our feeling of peace and security. On this framework, secondly, is patterned the *proper*, with its rich variety of changing prayers keynoted to fit days and feasts and seasons. The bulk of it is made up of the 150 psalms which are distributed over the week, and of readings from the treasury of the Bible and Christian literature suitable for each day.

To discuss the office in detail would require many volumes. Here, however, we shall content ourselves with considering the symbolism of the different sections of the office, their relationship to the structure of the Hours, and the way the symbols are governed by the rising and diminishing of each day's light.

2. Structure, theme, and symbol in the Hours

The most important key which opens up the treasures of meaning in the office is an awareness that the Hours belong to different times of the day. Originally, the recitation of these Hours was to be distributed over the day—one part to be said every three clock hours.

Such timely placement is not often practicable in our twentieth century schedules, but sometimes, perhaps during a vacation, those who say the office might experiment with the placing of the different sections in their appropriate times. In this way they become more meaningful. And always, whether prayed at that specific time or not, we can have in our minds the images proper to whatever Hour we are saying, and pray it as a blessing on the part of the day it is meant to transfigure.

Here is the time schedule of the Hours in summary. We will talk about the themes and symbols of the different Hours immediately after this. You will notice that the Hours are mostly named according to the ancient way of telling time; for example, *Prime* means the first hour of the day. It comes at our six o'clock in the morning. We get our word *primary* from the same stem.

Office begins at midnight; this Hour is Matins. It blesses the three hours which begin at midnight. Then comes Lauds (meaning *praise*), which belongs to three in the morning, the dawn hour; Prime for six, the beginning of the work day; Terce (the third hour) is at nine o'clock, the hour of the descent of the Holy Spirit on Pentecost; Sext (the sixth hour), at noontide, when Christ hung suspended between heaven and earth; None (the ninth hour), three in the afternoon, the time when the shadows grow long; Vespers (the name means the *evening star*), six o'clock, time for the evening meal and the evening sacrifice of praise; Compline, nine o'clock, time for resting securely under the loving care of God.

Let us look at these Hours in a little more detail. Matins is the first. When the sun is down out of sight, buried in the sea or behind the hills, and the earth is resting in quiet darkness, then is the time for the midnight Hour of Matins.

It is a quiet contemplative time and a quiet contemplative prayer: "O Lord, our Lord, how glorious is thy name in all the earth. . . . When I gaze at the heavens, the work of thy fingers, the moon and stars which thou hast made" (Ps. 8, Sunday at Matins, p. 36).[52] As man is awed into silence when he goes into the woods at night, and as the night-prowling and night-flying beasts and birds are especially quiet of movement, so the feeling of Matins is one of silence and stillness.

In this silence is a note of listening and watching—a kind of anticipation. Just as one is calmed, yet rests in tranquil expectation of dawn, when one wakes in the dark and hears the ocean beat on the rocks, or looks up into a soft black sky, so the Hour of Matins is an anticipation of the dawn. It looks forward to the morning's Mass which will bring Christ the Bridegroom to the waiting Christian. "If thou searchest my heart, if thou visitest me in the night . . . thou wilt not find sin in me. . . . But I in justice shall see thy face, awaking, I shall be satisfied with the sight of thee" (Ps. 16, Mon. at Matins).

This is the hour to watch. And even if we are ordinarily asleep at this time, still by uniting ourselves prayerfully to the spirit of Matins before we go to sleep we can truthfully say, like the beloved in the Song of Songs: "I sleep and my heart watches." We watch because we do not wish the Lord to come like a thief in the night, and find us with lamps burned out, unprepared for his coming.

The structure of Matins, in broad outline, consists of four sections: 1) an invitation to praise God; 2) a hymn giving the theme of the Hour; 3) three parts called *nocturns,* each consisting of three psalms followed by three lessons (short readings from scripture or other Christian literature); 4) the triumphant hymn, *Te Deum*. Such is the basic structure; slight variations occur at times.

One of the particularly interesting features of Matins is the first, the *invitatory*—an invitation to praise God. It is always phrased in the words of Psalm 49: "Come let us rejoice unto the Lord, let us shout with joy to the rock of our salvation; let us come into his presence with praises, with songs let us rejoice unto him."

Between each verse of this unchanging psalm, however, the office introduces short phrases—keynotes which suit the different days. Thus in its very introduction, the artistic principle of unity in variety is carried out. By such devices, moreover, we are kept attuned to the variations of weekdays, feasts, and seasons.

Such a single sentence or phrase keynoting a psalm or canticle is called an *antiphon*. It is something like the signature which gives the key in music. Just as the key signature shows the musician where, on his keyboard, to play the music; and the music itself sounds different in various keys; so the antiphon directs our minds to pray the psalm with a certain meaning uppermost; and the same psalm takes on quite a different character when it is keynoted by a different antiphon.

Let us look at three of these invitatory antiphons which strike the note for three widely different feasts. On Ascension Day we find, "Alleluia, Christ, the Lord, ascending into heaven, Come, let us adore, Alleluia" (Spring vol., p. 489). Because this is a feast celebrating Christ's glorious ascension, where he takes his place at the right hand of the Father, therefore we adore him as he is placed before our eyes in the conditions of this mystery.

Again, during the office said to commemorate the dedication of a church, the antiphon is: "Holiness becometh the house of God; in her let us adore Christ her Bridegroom" (Spring, p. 155*), and our honor is accorded here both to our

Lord himself and to the Church whom he loves as a bridegroom loves his bride.

Finally, the note of our expected resurrection is given on All Souls' Day—the day on which we pray for all those who have died and are in purgatory: "The King, for whom all things live, Come, let us adore" (Autumn, p. 661). Here our thoughts turn to Christ who is the resurrection and the life, and we adore him thankfully because he will restore to life us and all those souls who have gone before us into the kingdom of death.

These key thoughts are intended to rest warmly in the back of our minds while we recite the familiar invitatory psalm. By their presence to our thoughts they bring out new meanings in the psalm and make specific our purpose in saying it.

This principle of variation is one of the fascinating features of the office. For a further example of this same kind of procedure, let us look at the endings of Vespers. The evening Hour of Vespers always closes with Mary's *Magnificat*: "My soul doth magnify the Lord" (Luke 1:46 ff.). But the unchanging recitation of this canticle is always varied, because the Magnificat is begun and ended with some thought appropriate to the day's commemoration. Here are two of the Magnificat antiphons.

"I am the shepherd of sheep; I am the way, and the life; I am the good shepherd, and I know my sheep, and mine know me, alleluia" (Second Sun. after Easter). The Mass of this day presents the gospel of the Good Shepherd. The office carries on the theme. Following this antiphon, we are ready to adopt Mary's song of praise as our own and lose ourselves in admiration of the fact that Christ is truly our shepherd and we are his flock, well loved and guarded. This is the great thing which the Lord has done for us, and for which we praise him here in this day's Magnificat.

Then again, on Pentecost Sunday, we set the keynote for

our Magnificat by a thought of the Spirit's coming in the sign of fire: "Today were the days of Pentecost ended, alleluia: today the Holy Ghost appeared, in the form of fire..." We are rejoicing here because we too have seen the coming of Pentecost and the Holy Spirit's fire has also descended on us.

Next after the invitatory comes the second feature of Matins, the hymn, which is changeable with days and seasons, but usually speaks of night and darkness (in keeping with the midnight hour), and of our rising from sleep in anticipation of our final resurrection with Christ; for example:

> Now from the slumbers of the night arising
> Chant we the holy psalmody of David.
> (Sundays after Pent., Summer)

or again:

> Hail, day! whereon the One in Three
> First formed the earth by sure decree.
> The day its Maker rose again,
> And vanquished death, and burst our chain.
>
> Away with sleep and slothful ease!
> We raise our hearts and bend our knees
> And early seek the Lord of all,
> Obedient to the prophet's call.
> (Sundays after Sept. 28.)

In both these examples, the theme of sleep and rising in the night to pray is apparent, and our rising is linked by anticipation with the theme of the next Hour, Lauds, which is dedicated to Christ's resurrection.

The third section of Matins is divided into three parts called nocturns. Each nocturn contains three psalms and three readings called lessons. Possibly the scripture readings and other lessons are placed here because night is particularly suitable for quiet contemplative thought.

Those who rise at night to pray sometimes feel "time ravel thin about them." And possessing this sense of the thinning out of time, this tranquil leisure, they may find that the inspired word takes special hold of the soul. At such times all our powers are quieted and we can remain peacefully centered on God: "Be still and know that I am God," as the psalmist says. And St. John of the Cross, the great poet and contemplative, uses the phrase as a recurrent theme in his discussions of prayer.

Matins can, in this way, transfigure all our quietude in God's presence: our sleep if we go to rest with the thought that "I sleep and my heart watches," and our times of quiet prayer and reading whether done at night time or in the day.

When the nocturns are finished, Matins concludes with the traditional chant of praise and thanksgiving, the *Te Deum*, "We praise thee, O God; we acknowledge thee to be the Lord." This chant has been sung for hundreds of years on occasions of public rejoicing such as a deliverance from danger, victory over enemies, or other great favors received from God. It is a concentrated outburst of praise of God, the natural fruit of the contemplative quiet of Matins. In this ringingly triumphant hymn all the earth, the heavens, all the angels, cherubim and seraphim are urged to cry out, "Holy, Holy, Holy!"

Usually Matins is followed immediately by the next Hour which is Lauds. Matins is, as we have seen, rather long. It begins at midnight and continues for some time, hence the interval before time for Lauds at three, would be quite short. For this reason the office is often spoken of as having seven Hours, since Matins and Lauds are counted as one. The psalmist's words, therefore, "Seven times a day I give praise unto thee," are appropriately used in describing the office prayers as they are distributed over the day. In their meaning, however, they make up eight Hours—consecrating each three hours throughout the circle of twenty-four.

At the time of Lauds, which is dawn, the quiet anticipation of Matins begins to wake to a greater eagerness. The sun will soon be rising, the birds will begin to sing, all the world's inhabitants will stir once more. We remember that it was at dawn that Christ rose on the first Easter. We, ourselves, will rise today from the "little death" of sleep, so that we may go out into this new day of grace. And all nature, too, wakes and rises from its night's quietude.

Most of all, we anticipate two resurrections—two appearances of the risen Christ to us. The first will be in the morning's Mass, when he will be in the midst of us, as he came through closed doors into the midst of his disciples on the first Easter. And the second will be our death, when we will see him face to face. The Church also anticipates the coming of her bridegroom, Christ, at the end of the world, when the number of her members will be complete, and there will be no more sorrow. Lauds thus consecrates all wakings and sunrises and new beginnings.

Basically, the structure of Lauds falls into five parts (we shall see later that Vespers parallels this structure): 1) five psalms, each introduced and concluded by an antiphon suited to the day; 2) a very short reading related to the Mass of the day; 3) a hymn which speaks of dawn; 4) a proper prayer—the collect from the day's Mass; 5) Zachary's song of praise, the *Benedictus* (Luke 1:68-79): "Blessed be the Lord, the God of Israel, because he has visited and wrought redemption for his people . . ."

Since Lauds celebrates the imminent coming of Christ in the Mass, the Benedictus, which is a song of joy over the birth of John the Baptist, is especially appropriate. This is so, because John was the one who *made ready* for Christ. He is the one who goes before Christ, as Lauds goes before the coming of Christ in the Mass. Like the Magnificat which we discussed above, the Benedictus also has its own antiphons which are full of meaning and light.

First let us look at sections one (psalms), three (hymn), and five (Benedictus), because these parts of Lauds carry the two themes of praise for sunrise and resurrection, and our longing for Christ to come in the Mass. United with this longing, is also our desire that we may one day rise from our death and be with the risen Christ in his glory.

In section one, the five psalms are frequently chosen for their note of praise—and the word Lauds means praise. Moreover, the whole earth is drawn into this praise by the use here of many symbols taken from earth's spaciousness and fruitfulness, air's storm and breezes, fire's heat and brightness, water's power of fructifying and destroying.

Here are some examples of such praise and such symbols from the four elements. The quotations are from Lauds for Sundays (Spring, pp. 47 ff.). "The Lord reigns, he is clothed with majesty . . . he has established the whole world which shall not be moved. . . . The floods lift up, O Lord, the floods lift up their thunder" (Ps. 92:1-3). "Rejoice unto the Lord, all ye lands; serve the Lord with gladness . . . Know ye that the Lord is God: he made us and we are his, his people and the sheep of his pasture" (Ps. 99:1-3).

And a little further on we see: "Praise him, O sun and moon, praise him, all ye shining stars. . . . Praise the Lord from the earth, ye sea-monsters and all ye depths of the sea, fire and hail, snow and mist, stormy wind, that fulfills his word" (Ps. 148:3-8); "O ye seas and rivers, bless the Lord; O ye whales, and all that move in the waters. . . . O ye fire and heat, bless the Lord. . . . O ye mountains and hills, bless the Lord" (Dan. 3:65-79).

The repeated theme of praise is clear, and all the elements of earth are included in the praise: earth symbols related to extension in space—mountains and hills; fruitfulness in "sheep of his pasture"; air and fire in "fire and hail, snow and mist, stormy wind"; while references to water abound. No corner of the natural world fails to be transfigured by the stream of praise which rises to God's throne.

Again, the secondary theme of Lauds is an eager expectation, an ardent longing for the coming of Christ. The psalmist, for example, cries out (and we adopt his words): "O God, thou are my God: thee do I earnestly seek; My soul thirsts for thee, my flesh longs for thee, like a dry and thirsty land without water" (Ps. 62:1-3; Spring, 47).

The hymn, which is the third part of Lauds, also carries the note of resurrection and sunrise. Here is a selection from Eastertime Lauds:

> The morn had spread her crimson rays,
> When rang the skies with shouts of praise . . .
> He comes victorious from the grave,
> The Lord omnipotent to save. . . .
> With Christ we died, with Christ we rose,
> When at the font his name we chose . . .

And then the response which follows the hymn prolongs the thought in the words: "In thy resurrection, O Christ . . . let heaven and earth rejoice." Outside the Easter season the emphasis is placed on the dawn of day and our rising with fervor to sing God's praises.

The canticle, Benedictus, is the fifth part of Lauds, and though in its historical setting it belongs to the scenes of the Incarnation, for it is Zachary's song at the birth of John the Baptist (Luke 1:68-79), it also speaks of Christ as a sunrise—a dawn—"The Orient from on high [who will] enlighten those that sit in darkness." From this discussion of Lauds, parts one, three, and five, we can gain some notion of the way that the themes of dawn, resurrection, praise, and longing for the coming of Christ are made concrete for us in the poetry of the office.

It remains for us to recognize that parts two (the reading) and four (the proper prayer) remind us, not so much of the hour of the day, but rather of the special themes and images presented to us in the Mass of the day. By these reminders our powers are continually brought back to the Mass, which is central to our day. And in this way our life and all our being is unified in itself and directed anew to its goal of transfiguration into Christ—that same Christ whom we offer to the Father during our Mass.

We might say in this connection, that the Mass has contained in itself the fragrance, the sweet smelling incense of our best praise of God. And just as fragrances stir deeper memories than sights or sounds, so when these perfumes, these reminders during the day come and renew that first incense of the great sacrifice, they stir up our memories of God, and renew the joyful surrender to him which we made at Mass.

The four so-called Little Hours, of Prime (6:00 A.M.), Terce (9:00 A.M.), Sext (Noon), None (3:00 P.M.) are distributed over the working day and serve to draw our hearts with swift intent away from earthly concerns and give them a moment's rest in freedom in God.

Each is structured in three parts: 1) after the usual introductory aspiration comes the hymn which ordinarily keynotes the hour of the day; 2) an antiphon followed by three psalms which are concluded by the repetition of the antiphon; 3) the short reading (Little Chapter) and proper prayer (the Mass collect, usually).

Less than five minutes suffice to say one of these Hours, and five minutes' praise of God interposed between three-hour work periods can become a welcome respite.

Each of the Little Hours has its own characteristic theme and imagery. The hymn usually refers to the time of day which the Hour is meant to sanctify. Prime, for example, is the prayer before work. We ask that the Lord may "order our day and actions in his peace" (Spring, 23). It is as if at this time the Master of the vineyard gives us his blessing and tells us to go into his vineyard and bring forth fruit a hundredfold. The hymn mentions both the beginning of this new day, and the help we need in the day's occupations:

> Now in the sun's new dawning ray
> Lowly of heart, our God we pray
> That he from harm may keep us free
> In all the deeds this day shall see.
> (Spring, 17)

And then this hymn goes on to state the purpose for which we desire God's protection and help. It is in order that we may come at day's end once more to praise him in security and confidence:

> Then when the light of day is gone,
> And night in course shall follow on,
> We free from cares the world affords,
> May chant the praise that is our Lord's.

In the second section (the antiphon and three psalms), the antiphon itself usually reminds us of the day's feast or fast (as we have now grown to expect from the other Hours of the office). The psalms on the other hand, ordinarily have some connection with themes suitable for the day of the week.

Monday, for example, is the beginning of the week's work, and so we turn confidently to God for help. We hope that we "shall receive a blessing from the Lord," knowing that whatever he ordains for this journey, this procession into the new week will be right: "The ordinances of the Lord are right, making glad the heart. . . . They are more to be desired than gold, than much fine gold" (Ps. 18). Then we end the same psalm with a prayer that we may live the day holily: "May the words of my mouth and the thoughts of my heart be accepted in thy sight, O Lord, my Rock, and my Redeemer."

Then again, on Thursday, when we commemorate the Last Supper, and Christ's giving us his body and blood to be our heavenly banquet, the psalms remind us of this event. We find, therefore, the famous Psalm 22, with its references to refreshment and welcoming care and sharing of food, at Prime on Thursday:

> The Lord is my shepherd: I want for nothing; he makes me rest in green pastures.
> He leads me to waters where I may rest; he restores my soul. . . .
> Although I walk in a darksome valley, I shall fear no evil, for thou art with me.
> Thy crook and thy staff: these comfort me.
>
> Thou preparest a table for me before the eyes of my foes;
> Thou anointest my head with oil; my cup brims over.
> Goodness and kindness will follow me all the days of my life,
> And I shall dwell in the house of the Lord days without end.

From these examples it can be seen how the psalms of Prime pick up themes characteristic of the days of the week and present them to our minds.

This same plan is followed fairly consistently in the other three Little Hours (Terce, Sext, and None). A little practice in watching for such themes and images will open up a whole world of understanding and delight, and will enrich incalculably the tone of our prayer. These benefits can be ours whether we actually say the office itself, or only choose to distribute over our day a few suitable hymns or psalms from the riches of the Bible, missal, and office book.

The third section of each of the Little Hours, which consists of the short reading and proper prayer, reminds us of the day's Mass, again stirring our memories by a pervasive fragrance such as we have known during Lauds.

Since Terce (9:00), Sext (Noon), and None (3:00) in their second and third parts, that is psalms and reading with proper prayer, follow this same pattern we will not comment on each one separately. We will, rather, content ourselves with pointing out the way in which each hour's hymn strikes the characteristic note for that time of day.

The hymn, therefore, for Terce, is next. This hour of nine o'clock in the morning is the time of the descent of the Holy Spirit. We read in Acts 2, that when the apostles were all together, there appeared parted tongues of fire, and it rested on each of them, and "they were all filled with the Holy Spirit" (Acts 2:4).

Then they were invested with zeal and eloquence, and went out to preach to the people. But some, mocking, said "These men are full of new wine." Peter, however, answered that they were not drunk, as was supposed. It was too early in the morning: "It is but the third hour of the day." This hour is Terce, or nine o'clock, according to our reckoning.

Accordingly, the hymn for Terce is an invocation of the Holy Spirit. At this time we say what the Church is always saying to the Spirit: *"Veni*—Come." With insistence, Mother Church repeats, "Come—come now!" And in answer the Spirit comes down upon Christians in continually new Pentecosts.

This hymn is particularly beautiful, and would serve as a good prayer before work—especially any kind of intellectual work. All illuminations of our minds, all glimpses of truth, as well as all love for others, are consecrated by this Hour. Here is the hymn:

> Come, Holy Ghost, who ever one
> Art with the Father and the Son,
> It is the hour, our souls possess
> With thy full flood of holiness.
>
> Let flesh, and heart, and lips, and mind,
> Sound forth our witness to mankind;
> And love light up the mortal frame,
> Till others catch the living flame.
>   (Spring, 23)

In these eight lines we first call on the Spirit to come. Then we praise him because he is God, living with the Father and the Son in the great mystery of the Trinity. And the Trinity is the first and most wonderful example (if one may so speak in all reverence) of unity and variety—the perfect unity of one God; and the fruitful variety of three divine Persons, each with a different relationship to the others.

After praising him, we return insistently to our invitation: "It is the hour," we say. It is time. Therefore come and possess our souls. Light up all our being (flesh, and heart, and lips, and mind) with thy love, so that we may bear witness to thy divinity, and spread the living flame of thy love to others. When the hymn has been said, the rest of Terce (three psalms with antiphon, then reading with proper prayer) follows according to the pattern set by Prime, which we have already described.

The hymn for Sext, the sixth hour, or twelve o'clock noon, in our time, speaks of this period as "perfect day," that is, the time when the sun is at its zenith. We know that this is the hour when we commemorate Christ's nailing to the cross. Here he, like the sun, is on high—he is "lifted up"—and from him in his suffering, power radiates to save and transfigure the world and to draw all things to himself. We think, therefore, not only of his agony, but also of his triumph because by his death and resurrection he has won victory. Now death is swallowed up in victory, for the scars of death remaining in the body of Christ are glorified scars, which perpetually plead for us before the face of the Father.

This is the image which the Church presents for our contemplation during Sext. It is like the illustration which occurs in this book before chapter five. In it we see Christ—a Christ nailed to the cross, and therefore an image reminiscent of his sufferings and death; but a Christ, also, who wears the priestly robes of his power to mediate between us and God. At the same time these are the kingly robes of his ruling at the right hand of the Father, where (because he is a king), the Father anoints him "with the oil of gladness to be a priest for ever and king of the whole world" (Preface, Feast of Christ the King).

With None, three o'clock in the afternoon, the shadows begin to lengthen. It is a time of quiet and solemn thought. We are coming near the end of the day's work and we are tired. We realize that all things change; everything comes to an end. We think how our life, too, draws swiftly toward its close, and thinking these serious thoughts we pray in the hymn for None:

> O strength and stay upholding all creation,
> Who ever dost thyself unmoved abide,
> And day by day the light in due gradation
> From hour to hour through all its changes guide;
>
> Grant to life's day a calm unclouded ending,
> An eve untouched by shadows of decay,
> The brightness of a holy deathbed blending
> With dawning glories of the eternal day.
>
> (Spring, 27)

Thoughts of the transience of time and of God's steadfastness blend here, just as the imagery pictures the sunset of mortal life blending with an immortal dawn. While we watch the picture, we pray that our changing lives may come, after the evening of death to God's unchanging glory.

The psalms of None, in relation to this concept of the close of the day and of life, often present images of harvest—the bringing in of the sheaves which reward man's labor. Here is an example from None of the Little Office of the Blessed Virgin: "The Lord has done great things for us; we are become joyful! . . . They that sow in tears, shall reap in joy. Going they go and weep, carrying seed for sowing: Coming, they shall come with rejoicing carrying their sheaves" (Ps. 125, Winter, 130).

Two more Hours remain—the evening Hour of Vespers, and the Church's night prayer, Compline. Vespers receives its name from the evening star. It commemorates the time when the evening sacrifice was offered in the temple of Jerusalem, and so it serves as an echo of our Eucharistic Sacrifice. This is also the time of the evening meal. We therefore think of Christ's Last Supper with his disciples and his institution of the Holy Eucharist.

We are, further, reminded of a beautiful Hebrew custom which Mary may have observed, and which is continued to this day in Jewish households. This is the ceremony of the lighting of lamps in homes where the evening meal is ready and all wait for the gathering of the family around the table. It is the mother's place to light the lamps, and while she does it she prays a blessing on her family and her home.

For all these reasons it is peculiarly appropriate that Vespers should always end with the Magnificat. This is Mary's song of rejoicing because the Son of God was made a member of her home and family. He is her Son as well as God's.

The Magnificat, moreover, is also the canticle of Mother Church when she rejoices that the Lord is with her, too. He abides with her in the Eucharist, and lives through the lives of her members—those members who are so closely united with Christ that they have become hands for his work, feet for his journeys, and hearts on fire with zeal to spread the flame of his Spirit's love.

Paralleling the structure of Lauds, which was the other Hour devoted primarily to praise and thankfulness, Vespers also has a five-part structure: 1) five psalms, each keynoted with its own antiphon; 2) the reading of the day's short lesson; 3) the hymn and versicle; 4) the Magnificat with its antiphon; 5) the repetition of the prayer—the collect from the Mass of the day.

The five psalms frequently carry the theme of completion and harvest. This harvest theme was begun during None, as we have seen. There it was primarily a foretelling of harvest to come. And there is a further significant difference in the way the theme is presented in the two Hours. At None, the harvest is the reward of man's work in the fields; at Vespers, it is the fruitfulness of the family which is stressed. Here are two examples of such imagery: "He makes her who was barren, to dwell in a house, the joyful mother of children" (Ps. 112:9, Spring, 71); and also, "Praise the Lord, O Jerusalem . . . he has blessed thy children within thee. He has made peace in thy borders, with the marrow of wheat he fills thee" (Ps. 147:1-3).

Each kind of harvest is appropriate to its Hour, for None comes near the end of the work day, and Vespers depicts the family (Christ with his apostles; the mother and father with their children) gathered around the tables and partaking together of the evening meal.

Many images during Vespers also bring before our minds this thought of the evening meal—and in turn we come back to the Eucharist, and the fruitfulness which springs from our union with Christ. One of the most important of these occurs in the Magnificat: "He has filled the hungry with good things" (Luke 1:53).

The psalms of Vespers are especially worthy of study because of their Eucharistic references. As we said above, the Hallel psalms (113-118) which were said at the paschal meal—and the Last Supper was a paschal meal—are also used at Vespers. The word *Hallel* comes from Hallelujah (or alleluia), a word of rejoicing which occurs frequently in these psalms.

The second section of Vespers, the lesson of the day, as we now expect, is usually taken from the Mass; the third section (hymn and versicle) ordinarily refers to the season of the year; that is, to Lent, Easter, etc., rather than to the time of day as the hymns do in the Little Hours. We have already discussed the Magnificat, which is the climax of Vespers, along with some of its antiphons, earlier in this chapter. Finally, Vespers closes, as other Hours do, with the proper prayer from the Mass of the day.

The last Hour is Compline which consecrates the three hours following upon nine in the evening. Compline also has a five-part structure, consisting of : 1) some preliminary night prayers; 2) three psalms; 3) hymn; 4) reading and responses; 5) Canticle of Simeon, final night prayer, and blessing.

The keynote of Compline is: "May the Lord almighty grant us a quiet night and a perfect end." Before the Hour itself begins, this short aspiration is said as a kind of preparation, and with it is read a selection from I Peter (5:8-9), which describes the devil going about as a lion seeking someone to devour. The confiteor follows this.

Then for the second section, after this preparation, we have three psalms which are changeable. And in the third place comes the hymn which prays that God will guard the Christian from evil dreams and night time fears. This is followed by the prayer of our Lord on the cross: "Into thy hands, O Lord, I commend my spirit." This is a very appropriate aspiration for us at the time of retiring to rest. Along with this we say: "O Lord, keep us as the apple of thy eye; protect us under the shadow of thy wings" (Spring, p. 36).

Compline climaxes with the biblical canticle, the song of Simeon, as Matins climaxes with the Te Deum, Lauds with the Benedictus, and Vespers with the Magnificat. Here is the canticle which Simeon spoke when he met Mary and Joseph and the child Jesus in the temple (Luke 2:29-32):

> Now thou dost dismiss thy servant, O Lord, according to thy word in peace.
> Because my eyes have seen thy salvation,
> Which thou hast prepared before the face of all peoples,
> A light of revelation to the Gentiles, and a glory for thy people Israel.

And so, with the newborn Christ in Simeon's arms glowing like a light which we may set beside our beds—a lamp shining out to keep away the "terrors of the night . . . the pestilence that prowls in the darkness" (Ps. 90, Autumn, 59), we finish Compline by asking the Lord's protection.

For this purpose we invite the angels to dwell in our house: "Save us, O Lord, while we are awake, and guard us while we sleep: that we may watch with Christ and rest in peace" (Autumn, p. 26). "Visit, O Lord, this house, and drive far from it all snares of the enemy: let thy holy Angels dwell herein, who may keep us in peace" (Autumn, 27).

In this exploration of the office, several things have become apparent. One is that new delight comes to our days when we consciously share in the stream of prayer which flows to God all day long; another is that an awareness of the symbolism inherent in the different stages of light during the day and night enriches our whole outlook; and a third is that an admiring and intent gaze directed to the artistry of structure and symbol in the Church's official prayer, can inspire us to pray better.

This holds true whether we say the whole office, a part of it, a chosen psalm now and then, or whether we merely unite ourselves silently to the other members of Christ's mystical body, who pray the office for and with us. A few of our specific findings are summarized in the chart on the next page.

In the chapter which follows this one we shall examine the last and widest circle, the year. Here we shall be interested in the unified progression which shapes the whole cycle around the three great feasts of Christmas, Easter, Pentecost, and their interrelationships with each other.

Chart of the Office

Hour	Time Consecrated	Keynotes	Imagery
Matins	Midnight	Quiet contemplation and peaceful anticipation	Darkness; nature at rest
Lauds	3:00 A.M.	Praise; eager anticipation	Dawn; resurrection
Prime	6:00 A.M.	Day's work; "Go into my vineyard"	Planting of seed; all occupations
Terce	9:00 A.M.	Invitation to Holy Spirit: *Veni*	Wind and fire of Pentecost
Sext	12.00 Noon	Battle for Christ's triumph; also noontide rest	Sun at zenith; Christ on cross suffering and triumphant: drawing all to himself
None	3:00 P.M.	Longing for rest from day's work; for peaceful and happy death	Lengthening shadows; harvest; "It is finished," last words of Christ
Vespers	6:00 P.M.	Thankfulness at day's end; memories of Mass, the Eucharistic thanks; Mary's thanksgiving	Mother Church at home, lighting lamps; incense of evening sacrifice; Hour of Last Supper
Compline	9:00 P.M.	Confidence in God's protection	Setting in of dark; devil as a roaring lion; but Christ's, "I will gather thee as a hen gathers her chicks"

CHAPTER NINE

Of the Year: Fourth Circle

> Even in us the voices of seasons, the snuffle of winter, the song of spring, the drone of summer, the voices of beasts and birds, praise Thee.
>
> T. S. ELIOT [53]

AROUND ALL the circles of our repeated days and doings, turns the steady progression of the year, with the flare and pageantry of autumn, the swift winds of winter, the spring's surging new life in fields and woods, and the indolence of long hot summertime. Each season is new, but each season returns. And still every return is like a fresh creation; every season returns at a different time and in a different way. Witness the coming of spring. The calendar says it arrives on March twenty-first, but when does this ever happen? And when spring does come, is it ever like any season we have known before?

Each season, like every human being, is individual and unique: "It was all / Shining, it was Adam and maiden, / The sky gathered again / And the sun grew round that very day,"—this is the way Dylan Thomas [54] describes a boy's sense of the perennial newness in things. He feels that every new day brings the world back to him as fresh as at the beginning of creation.

When we remember the seasons, we think how wonderfully God planned their variation. He even tipped our round world so that it does not hang perfectly straight in space, but is placed so that its axis is diagonal. If the earth were not tipped slightly sidewise in this manner, we should miss the variation of spring and summer, fall and winter. How dreary to live in a world of unchanging weather. But we are in no danger of this, for God has provided four seasons in the natural year—each year we expect them, yet their recurrence does not pall. Somehow, summer always surprises us.

In the supernatural world there are seasons too, feasts and weeks in which we re-live the different mysteries in the life of Christ; or rather, times in which Christ re-lives his mysteries in us. For Christ is the center, the axis, on which the year turns. He is the "still point of the turning world" and around him everything revolves.

The natural world has four seasons, but in the supernatural world there are only three: three seasons centering around the three feasts of Christmas, Easter, Pentecost; characterized by the three thematic symbols of light, life, love; and enriched by subordinate patterns of imagery related to the main symbols.

Each of these seasons, as we have said, centers around one great feast: Christmas, the celebration of the nativity of our Lord, is the first one. This is the commemoration of the mystery of the Word's taking human flesh, of God's making himself visible to us in the form of a man.

Because he did this, "we had sight of his glory, glory such as belongs to the Father's only-begotten Son, full of grace and truth" (John 1:14). This season begins with Advent, about four weeks before Christmas, and continues through a profusion of feasts of light, until the brightness climaxes at Candlemas on February 2. Christmas is so predominantly a feast of light because it is the season which shows us "a Son who is the radiance of the Father's splendour" (Epistle, Third Mass, Christmas Day).

In the second season, the central feast is Easter, the celebration of Christ's and our passover or passage from death to life. For this reason, even though Easter continues the Christmas motif of light, still the dominant theme here is one of life coming out of death.

At this time each year, many people are baptized, and thus they, along with Christ, pass through the dark waters of death to self and rise to a new and different life oriented towards God. As St. Paul tells the Colossians: "You, by baptism, have been united with his burial, united too with his resurrection. ... God raised him from the dead. And in giving life to him, he gave life to you too" (Col. 2:12-13).

Each Christian, moreover, dies a kind of death during every Lent and Holy Week, and rises in a very real way with Christ at Easter. This truth is behind the prayer of Hopkins: "Let him easter in us, be a dayspring to the dimness of us." [55] The Easter season begins with Septuagesima Sunday, approximately seventy days before Easter, and concludes with the Ascension of Christ, forty days after the Resurrection.

Finally, the last of these feasts is Pentecost. Here the *light* of Christmas and the *life* of Easter come together and flame out in *love*. The Spirit of Love comes at Pentecost, and the motif of the whole season is love.

We know how Christ had promised his apostles another Comforter to take his place after the Ascension. He said: "I will ask the Father, and he will give you another to befriend you, one who is to dwell continually with you forever" (John 14:16-17). This is the Comforter who came at the first Pentecost. His season begins after the Ascension with ten days' preparation, and continues through a long series of Sundays, completing the circle of the year with the last Sunday after Pentecost.

The theme of this last Sunday is the end of time. And the

first Sunday of Advent, which follows immediately, takes up the same theme. In this interesting way, the liturgy shows the continuity of seasons by the repeated theme which carries over from one season into the other. "What we call the beginning is often the end / And to make an end is to make a beginning. The end is where we start from," as Eliot says in "Little Gidding."

At the same time, however, that the circle is being completed in this way, and begun again, the Church also encourages us to think of the event which will shatter the circle of time. This will happen with the second coming of Christ. Eternity will, with his coming, break through into time and scatter it in a blaze of glory, and then unite all once more in the perfect fulfillment of God's everlasting plans.

The seasons are three and yet they are one. They are one because their subject is one: Christ the center and his relationships with the world and with the Godhead. And they are one because their symbolism progresses from the dawn light of the Savior's birth, through his resurrection (and ours) to a new life, to the climax of love which flames out at Pentecost.

Each theme is dominant in its own season, but it is also carried over into the next. The light glowing out of darkness at Christmastide shines into Easter. It is not lost, but takes a secondary place in respect to the main theme of Easter, which is life coming out of death. And in similar fashion, both light and life are carried into the time of Pentecost. Here they unite and their union bears fruit in love.

However, the seasons are separate and varied, as well as unified, because each recalls a different set of mysteries. Each one, moreover, as we have seen, is built around a different theme or symbol. And supporting this, each has its own subordinate patterns of imagery: the brightness of sun and angels for Christmas; journeys at the beginning of Lent, when we commence our dark way toward death with Christ;

water and bread, two necessities of life, all through Easter time; wind and flame and especially harvest fruits at Pentecost.

Besides these diversities, each season has a key word which catches the spirit of the time and echoes through all its songs and prayers: *Gloria* for Christmas, from the song the angels sang to the shepherds at Bethlehem; *Alleluia*, the untranslatable cry of joy for the resurrection; and *Veni*, the word which invites the coming of the Holy Spirit. These key themes and images are summarized on the chart which follows.

CHART OF THE SEASONS

	Christmastide	*Easter*	*Pentecost*
Central event	Nativity	Resurrection	Coming of Holy Spirit
Preparation	Advent	Lent	Ten days after Ascension: Upper Room
Related days and seasons	Holy Innocents, Dec. 28; Circumcision and Holy Name; Epiphany; Presentation	Holy Week; Ascension	Many Sundays—life of mystical body of Christ
Theme	Light out of darkness	Life out of death	Love from union of life and light
Pattern	Upward; increasing light of revelation	Downward and then up; into death before resurrection	Steadily on in ever widening circles; growth of body of Christ
Images	Brightness of sun and angels	Journey; water and bread for life	Wind and flame of Spirit; harvest
Key word	*Gloria*	*Alleluia*	*Veni*

Let us now look at the Masses of the three seasons in turn, in order to see concretely the carrying out of the basic themes and ideas by means of symbolic images. For this, we shall confine ourselves to the texts of the seasonal Masses. It is true that the office also presents these same themes and symbols—sometimes in even more vivid fashion. But the missal furnishes more than enough material for our purposes.

1. *Christmastide*

> And the light shone in darkness and
> Against the Word the unstilled world
>   still whirled
> About the centre of the silent Word.
>
>   T. S. ELIOT [56]

Christmas, for its central idea, presents the thought of a gradual revelation of the Word made flesh who is the light of the world. Repeatedly we hear such phrases as: "Out of Sion, in perfect beauty God comes revealed" (Gradual, 2 Sun. Advent), or "By the grace of thy coming, light up the darkness of our minds" (Collect, 3 Sun. Advent).

This impression of dawning light ("The night is far on its course; the day draws near"—Epistle, 1 Sun. Adv.) is owing first of all to the dogma of the incarnation which is commemorated here. It was at the incarnation that the Second Person of the Trinity took a human nature, and so was made visible to us on our own terms. From being pure Spirit, he became a man who walked and slept and talked with other men. Because of his incarnation, therefore, we recognize that "through the mystery of the Word made flesh [God's] splendour has shone before our mind's eye with a new radiance" (Preface, Christmas).

This revelation is well imaged in the continual references to light. Symbols of light in general occur more than twenty-two times. Here are two examples: "He will bring to light what is hidden in darkness" (Epistle, 4 Sun. Advent), and again, "I the fashioner of darkness, the creator of light . . ." (Lesson, Ember Sat. Adv.).

Then there are the instances where the liturgy uses the imagery of the sun; for example, "See where the sun is . . . the sun which comes out as a bridegroom" (Gradual, Ember Sat. Advent). And finally we find the shining images of angels recurring again and again—such images as the following: "Thou who art enthroned above the Cherubim, reveal thyself" (Gradual, Christmas Eve). At least twelve sun symbols, and twenty references to angels are found in the Masses of this season.

Christmastide begins, as has been said, with Advent. The spirit of Advent is one of eager anticipation of the dawn. Hence comes a prevalence of future tenses, and of imperatives which call upon the Savior to hasten his coming; "Come, and smile upon us, Lord" (Introit, Ember Sat. Adv.), and "See where the Lord comes, with all his saints about him; glorious the light that the day will bring" (Communion, Ember Sat.)

In keeping with this eager expectancy are the many beautiful passages from Isaias, for example: "A message from the Lord: the barren desert thrills with rejoicing; the wilderness takes heart, and blossoms, fair as the lily. Blossom on blossom, it will rejoice and sing for joy. . . . All alike shall see the glory . . . of our God. . . . See where your Lord is . . . coming to save you! Then the eyes of the blind will be opened, and deaf ears unsealed; the lame man, then, will leap as the deer leap, the speechless tongue will cry aloud" (Lesson 2, Emb. Sat.). And there is, of course, the frequently repeated, "Send dew from above, you heavens, and let the skies pour down upon us the rain we long for, him, the Just One."

Like a refrain, the references to the sun and to angels occur all through this time. We see the sun from the gospel of the first Sunday of Advent where Christ tells of the failing of the sun and moon and stars before the coming of a greater Light, through five or six places where Christ is shown as symbolized by the sun in words like those which follow.

"Here at one end of heaven, the Sun has its starting place, and its course reaches to the other. . . . Where the sun is, there he sets up his tabernacle" (Grad. I and II, Emb. Sat.). Also related to these are the images of skies and of dawn: "See how the skies proclaim God's glory" (Introit, Ember Wed.): and also, "The kindness of God, our Saviour, has dawned on us" (Epistle, 2 Mass, Christmas).

Even more prevalent than symbols based on the sun, are those related to the angels. There are, for example, angels in the gospel narratives. On Ember Wednesday in Advent, for instance, is told the story of Gabriel's coming to Mary to announce that she was to be the mother of God. The coming of the angel to enlighten Joseph about the divinity of Mary's child is recounted on Christmas eve.

And in the first Mass of Christmas day we find the angel who "stood by [the shepherds when] the glory of the Lord shone about them." Then finally, Holy Innocents' Day (Dec. 28), which commemorates the children who were killed by Herod when he sought the Christ child, brings the account of the angel who warned Joseph to flee with the child and his mother into Egypt.

Angels appear, not only in the gospels, but in other parts of the Masses as well. Christ himself is compared to them: "His name shall be the Angel of Great Counsel" (Int., 3 Mass, Christmas). He is "superior to the angels. . . . Let all the angels of God worship before him. . . . He will have his angels be like the winds, the servants that wait on him like a flame of fire" (Epistle, 3 Mass, Christmas). All such images of bright beings like the sun and angels are present in profusion from the beginning of the Christmas season to the end. But it is now time for us to look at the feasts which follow Advent.

After Advent, comes Christmas day itself. On Christmas, the light which has been dawning during Advent, shines out first of all to those around the crib—to Mary and Joseph and the shepherds. While this light is beautiful, it has not yet reached out to all those who will come within its radius.

During this time, the collects and secrets are particularly glowing; in them we pray in this fashion: "God who hast made this most sacred night glow with the radiance of the true light . . . grant that we may share to the full in heaven the joys of that Light whom we have known sacramentally on earth" (Collect, 2 Mass, Christmas). Then finally comes the prayer which we discussed at length in chapter three of this book: "As this day's new-born human child shone with the brightness of the Godhead, so may the earthly substance of our offering bring the divine within our reach" (Secret, 2 Mass, Christmas).

On Christmas day, as we have suggested above, the Light shines out especially to those close around the crib—Mary and Joseph and the shepherds. We know the story of how Joseph and Mary had come from Nazareth to Bethlehem, and while they were there "she brought forth a son. . . . In the same country there were shepherds awake in the fields. . . . And all at once an angel of the Lord came and stood by them. . . . Behold the news I bring you is good news of a great rejoicing" (Gospel, 1 Mass, Christmas).

Even the Jewish ceremony of the circumcision of the child, which we commemorate on January 1, has meaning for this progressive revelation. On the one hand, it is a beginning of the theme of sacrificial suffering and finally death, which will come to the foreground at Easter time. But on the other hand, part of the ceremony was the giving of a name to the Child. This aspect is given a separate commemorative day on the Sunday after the Circumcision.

By the social act of naming a child, any child, he becomes known. He, as it were, requires a recognizable identity. With the Jews especially, this was a ceremony of acceptance by society, of recognition. It was an initiation into the nation of God's people. In this way, therefore, the Light shines out, not only to Christ's immediate family and friends as at the nativity; but also to all of God's people, the Israelites.

Then with the coming of the Wise Men, the light was to go to the distant places of the earth. These men had come to Jerusalem inquiring about the birthplace of a new king of the Jews. They were told to go to Bethlehem, and as they set out "the star which they had seen in the East was there going before them. . . . They, when they saw the star, were glad beyond measure; and so, going into that dwelling, they found the child there, with his mother Mary, and fell down to worship him." Afterwards they "returned to their own country" (Gospel, Epiphany).

This was the function of the Magi, to see Christ the light, and then to return home carrying the news of his coming to their countries. "By the leading of a star" (Collect, Epiphany), the Wise Men came; and the Church, thinking of this, sings a beautiful song from the prophecies: "Rise up, Jerusalem, and shine forth; thy dawn has come, and the glory of the Lord has broken upon thee. Darkness may envelop the earth, and all the nations lie in gloom; but upon thee the Lord shall dawn, over thee his splendour shall be revealed. Those rays of thine shall light the Gentiles on their path" (Lesson, Epiphany).

Finally, the climax of the light symbolism is reached with the feast of the presentation of our Lord in the temple. Mary and Joseph "brought Jesus up to Jerusalem, to present him before the Lord there." "At this time there was a man named Simeon living in Jerusalem. . . . The Holy Spirit was upon him: and by the Holy Spirit it had been revealed to him that he was not to meet death until he had seen that Christ whom the Lord had anointed. . . . And when the child Jesus was brought in by his parents . . . Simeon too was able to take him in his arms."

Then Simeon, holding the child, sang the canticle which describes our Lord as "the Light which shall give revelation to the Gentiles, [the] glory of thy people Israel" (Gospel, Candlemas). Simeon held the child up—as a light, as a candle —revealing the glory of God.

This feast is also called Candlemas, and on this day there are special blessings for candles. They, as is well known, are apt symbols for Christ who was the light which "shines in darkness" (Gospel, 3 Mass, Christmas); the light, who said of himself, "I am the light of the world.... He who follows me can never walk in darkness" (John 8:12).

As its name suggests, this is above all a feast of lights. In the blessing of candles, which precedes the Mass, there are at least eighteen references to light and fire. After the candles are blessed, the people go up to the altar and take them in their hands. These are the people "whose wish it is to carry these lights in their hands in honor of thee and to praise thee in song" as the Church says.

The lights are then carried in procession and their brightness is held up to shine during the Mass, at the gospel, when the story of Simeon is recounted, and during the portion of the Mass wherein Christ the light actually becomes present; that is, from the beginning of the Canon, through the Communion.

Thomas Merton [57] has a poem which describes this procession. In it he says,

> Look kindly, Jesus, where we come,
> New Simeons, to kindle
> Each at Your infant sacrifice his own
>   life's candle.
>   . . . .
> It is for this we come,
> And, kneeling, each receive one flame:
> *Ad revelationem gentium.* . . .

The poem is saying that these candles are put into our hands just as the revelation of Christ's divinity was given to the

Magi and to Simeon, and is given to us—in order that we may show forth the light to the peoples of the world. Our flame is to be *"Ad revelationem gentium*—For a revelation to the people." In this way, the light is carried now by us, and shines out in the contemporary world—even to the people who live in this twentieth century.

While we carry the flame of Christ's light, as the same poem says, it should be our aim, not to

> ... burn with brown and smoky flames, but bright
> Until our sacrifice is done,
> (By which not we, but You are known)
> And then, returning to our Father, one by one,
> Give back our lives like wise and waxen lights.

With this flaming out of light, the Christmas season ends, and we begin to prepare for Easter.

2. *Easter time*

> "A master of men was the Goodly Fere,
> A mate of the wind and sea.
> If they think they ha' slain our Goodly
>   Fere
> They are fools eternally.
>
> "I ha' seen him eat o' the honey-comb
> Sin' they nailed him to the tree."
>
> EZRA POUND [58]

Christmastide, as we have seen, proceeds gradually but unwaveringly upward, towards a climax of revelation and a culmination of lights. Easter time forms quite a different pattern. It must first go down, before it can come up. With Septuagesima, for example, the first Sunday of the season, a beginning is made in fear of death. The Introit starts the Mass with a note of fear: "Death's terrors were near at hand, the terror of the grave was all about me."

Here the voice is that of Christ, who in his mystical body is preparing to go once more into the chasm of death. It is also the voice of each one of us, who will go along with him through the purifying penance and compassion of Lent, down into the darkness of Good Friday, before we can come up from the grave on Easter Sunday.

From Septuagesima, then, the large pattern proceeds downward towards the purifying waters of the symbolic death of baptism. On our way we go through the penance and almsgiving of Lent, and through a sharing in Christ's sufferings by our compassion. This line reaches its nadir, its lowest level, on Good Friday. (Even here, however, the tone of the liturgy is by no means one of gloom. The Church never forgets that he "who trod the wine press alone" also rose in radiant life.)

After Good Friday, the line of our pattern turns swiftly upward, for with the Easter vigil we renew our baptismal vows, and thus "birth comes . . . from water and from the Holy Spirit" (John 3:5). Now we are transformed "into beings wholly new" (Postcomm., Easter Wed.). From Easter to Ascension, the line of our pattern moves along peacefully and joyously, curving gradually upward, until at Ascension it is lost to sight in the heavens.

We live, during these forty days, through hours of friendly companionship with the risen Christ. And then we come at Ascension to stand with the apostles and watch as he goes up to the right hand of the Father. As St. Mark tells the story, "And so the Lord Jesus, when he had finished speaking to them, was taken up into heaven, and is seated now at the right hand of God" (Gospel, Ascension). Then gladly we sing: "God goes up, loud are the cries of victory, the Lord goes up, loudly the trumpets peal" (Alleluia verse, Ascen.).

In this mystery, we cannot properly say that there is an increase of life, yet it is true to say that in it Christ's human nature receives an access of glory. It is now that the Father answers the prayer which Christ made at the Last Supper: "Now, Father do thou exalt me at thy own side, in that glory which I had with thee before the world began" (John 17:5).

The apostles, at the Transfiguration, had had a glimpse of this glory—but it passed very quickly. As Guardini says in *The Lord*, "The transfiguration was the summer lightning of the coming resurrection." [59] And the fullness of the resurrection glory comes to Christ with the ascension. In his petition, our Lord asks the Father that he may come to him, and sit at his right hand, even with his human nature. And it is this human nature which receives the special access of glory at the ascension.

Before Christ came to earth and took our humanity for his own, he was always with his Father. And while his incarnation did not separate him from the Father, nor deprive him of the beatific vision, yet his human body was on earth. Therefore, in a certain sense, we can say that the ascension did add something to the human nature of Christ—an increase of glory.

This mystery, moreover, sets the seal of the Father's approval upon all his earthly life. And we know that Christ desired this accolade, for he prayed that it might come to pass. Henceforward, Christ "sits forever at the right hand of God, offering for our sins a sacrifice that is never repeated" (Offertory, Mass of our Lord's High Priesthood). Now "his full achievement [is] reached" (Hebr. 5:9).

The Easter theme is, as we have said, life springing up out of death. At least three subordinate patterns of imagery support and enrich the theme. These are, after Septuagesima, through the early part of Lent, the imagery of journeys; and throughout the whole season, images of food, especially bread, which reminds us of the Eucharist, and fish which reminds us that the apostles were to become fishers of men. The imagery of water is also to be found in many places, and both bread and water are necessities of life—that life which is the dominant theme of the Easter season.

All three of these are interrelated. Man's going into the world which is on the other side of death has always been symbolized by the imagery of journeys. We remember how Homer, Virgil, and Dante describe their heroes' travels into the otherworld. With Septuagesima, we meditate on Christ the hero who is hastening his journey to death; and we too set out on a journey of death to our old selves—a death which is to issue in a life renewed in Christ. We, then, like Christ and with him, journey towards his death and resurrection.

Another symbol for this passage through death to life is that of plunging into water (as if one were being drowned) and then coming up again. For this reason we say that the water symbolism is related to that of the journey. The significance of the water, moreover, brings to our minds the cleansing, death dealing, and life renewing qualities of this element. How often, in this latter connection, have we come from a refreshing bath feeling not only cleansed, but as if we were somehow re-made. And, too, how often we have seen barren land grow green when water comes and causes seeds to spring to life.

In connection with these ideas, we think of our Lord's words: "A grain of wheat must fall into the ground and die, or else it remains nothing more than a grain of wheat; but if it dies, then it yields rich fruit" (John 12:24). From this combination of concepts: a journey into death, an invigorating bath, the death of the seed that it may live, the springing of life from apparently dead seed because of water, the use of the seed's fruit to furnish food for other life—from all these the Easter symbols come.

And to show how natural this connection of ideas is to the mind of men, think of the ancient pagans who believed in the effectiveness of a god who would go into a symbolic death, and come up alive, bringing fruitfulness to crops. They thought that if the god of growing things were to be drowned or buried, he would, like a seed planted, come up in spring bringing a rich harvest of grain.

Now Christ, as we have seen many times in this book, made it a practice to start from wherever he found men—he used the materials, the ideas, the people he found at hand, cleansed them from error (if errors were there) and then, by using them for his own purposes he transfigured them.

It is, therefore, not surprising to find that he should use the natural symbol of a going down into the earth or into the waters, for his supernatural purposes—endowing the symbol with deepened significance and completely different power. Besides, if God uses the prophecies of the sacred scriptures to foretell the mysteries of Christ's life, it is also possible for him to allow natural symbols to prophesy him in their own dim and far off way.

As we know, Christ talked of the spiritual significances of water long before he instructed the apostles to go out and baptize. At one time, for example (as St. John tells the story in chapter four of his gospel), Jesus came to a Samaritan city, "and there was a well there called Jacob's well. There, then, Jesus sat down, tired after his journey, it was about noon. And when a Samaritan woman came to draw water, Jesus said to her, Give me some to drink."

The woman could not understand how a man who was a Jew would speak to a woman who was a Samaritan. But our Lord said: "If thou knewest what it is God gives, and who this is that is saying to thee, Give me drink, it would have been for thee to ask him instead, and he would have given thee living water."

Again, the woman is puzzled. But Christ does not put her at ease by explaining his words on a purely natural level. He rather insists on their supernatural meaning. "Jesus answered her. Anyone who drinks such water as this will be thirsty again afterwards, the man who drinks the water I give him will not know thirst any more. The water I give him will be a spring of water within him, that flows continually to bring him everlasting life."

Interestingly, this account comes in the same chapter with some discussion of the baptism of John, and the preceding chapter (3) also has to do with water, for it records Christ's conversation with Nicodemus, which we have quoted before.

In all these cases, a natural element, with natural significances, was invested with supernatural meaning. We know that grace builds on nature. And nature herself supplies us with the materials for these Easter symbols of a journey through death into life, a going down into water and being "drowned" in order that one may come up renewed, a being cast into the earth to die as the seed dies in order to bring forth fruit. These symbols refer to Christ in his passion and resurrection, and they refer to our Christian life also.

Let us look at some of the Mass texts in order to follow these symbols. Among accounts of journeys, we have St. Paul's summary of the events of Exodus on Septuagesima Sunday: "Our fathers were hidden all of them under the cloud and found a path . . . through the sea; all alike, in the cloud and in the sea, were baptized into Moses' fellowship."

Here we see that Paul considers the Hebrews' exodus as a journey towards their baptism "into Moses' fellowship"; as our journey into Lent is a wayfaring toward the renewal of that baptism by which we were first received into fellowship with Christ.

With the next Sunday (Sexagesima), comes Paul's account of his own travels: "What journeys I have undertaken, in danger from rivers, in danger from robbers, in danger from my own people, in danger from the Gentiles. . . . I have met with toil and weariness, so often been sleepless, hungry and thirsty; so often denied myself food, gone cold and naked" (Epistle, Sexagesima). Our Lenten journey, too, is supposed to be like Paul's—a way of some toil and weariness and hunger.

Not only in the epistles, however, do we find journeys, but in many other places. Here are some examples: "Do thou maintain my steps firm in thy own ways, never allowing my feet to stumble" (Offertory, Sexagesima); and again in the Quinquagesima gospel we find: "Now we are going up to Jerusalem. . ." It is in this gospel that Christ tells the apostles plainly that this is a journey into death.

Then once more we hear, "Blessed are they, who pass through life's journey unstained" (Introit, Thurs., Passion Week), and at the prayer for the blessing of palms: "Grant that we may prepare for [Christ] a path of faith." This Sunday, Palm Sunday, of course, commemorates Christ's journey into Jerusalem riding on the beast of burden, with the people acclaiming him: "Hosanna to the Son of David." The revisions of the liturgy by our Holy Father, Pope Pius XII, emphasize this journey symbolism by stressing the procession with palms.

Even more important than the imagery of journeys, and continuing with increasing frequency up to the very day of the Ascension, are images of food and water. Water is used in three significant ways, to symbolize three things: 1) cleansing ("Lord, may this offering wash away our sins"—Secret, Quinquagesima); 2) death ("See how the waters close about me, threatening my very life"—Antiphon, Ash Wed.); 3) life ("Thou wilt be as secure as a well-watered garden, as a spring whose waters never fail"—Lesson, First Sat. in Lent).

Such symbolism of water continues throughout the season, and reaches its climax, as we have said, on Easter Saturday. In the Easter Vigil service of this day, the key to the baptismal symbols is found in the idea of the Holy Spirit like a great bird brooding over the original chaos to bring life out of it. We have noticed the Church's use of this symbol before —this picture of the time when "Earth was still an empty waste, and darkness hung over the deep; but already, over its waters, brooded the Spirit of God" (Gen. 1:2).

The Easter Vigil ceremony picks up this theme and embellishes it in several ways; for example: "O God, even at the beginning of the world, thy Spirit stirred the water that it might conceive the power of hallowing. . . . May the Spirit impregnate this water, prepared for the rebirth of men, by the secret inpouring of his divinity, that there may be born from the stainless womb of this divine font a new creation . . . the children of heaven" (*The Easter Vigil*, St. John's Abbey, 1952). This whole ceremony is filled with beauty, and will repay meditation made on it with increased understanding of our baptismal graces.

This Genesis symbol of the Dove brooding over the waters has inspired other poets as well. Milton, for example, in *Paradise Lost*, prays that the Spirit will instruct him—thou who

> . . . . from the first
> Wast present, and with mighty wings outspread
> Dove-like sat'st brooding on the vast abyss
> And mad'st it pregnant: what in me is dark
> Illumine.[60]

According to Genesis, one of the first things made was light. And here Milton asks the Spirit to create the light of inspiration in him.

Hopkins, in different fashion, pictures the earth as warmed by the great brooding Bird of the Holy Spirit who brings light up out of the darkness of each night:

> And though the last lights off the black West went
> Oh, morning, at the brown brink eastward, springs—
> Because the Holy Ghost over the bent
> World broods with warm breast and with ah! bright
> wings.[61]

The world is *bent* because it is sinful and sorrowful and hence out of shape. And it is also bent or curved like an egg which lies there under the wings of the Spirit. It is an egg which is warmed by the living, hovering Spirit. In it, new life grows, and will at last come forth as Christ burst from his tomb.

Besides the symbols of journeys and of water, the season of Easter is also filled with references to food. In part, these are planned to stir up our awareness of the great gift which Christ gave at the Last Supper—the gift which is his own living body and blood under the appearance of food. After the resurrection, this emphasis on food is especially marked, for in nearly every apparition of the risen Savior, he shares food with the disciples.

On the level of literal statement, Lent is full of allusions to fasting from food. Such prayers as the following set the scene for the season's penance: Grant [that] thy faithful . . . may enter upon . . . the fast . . . and pass through it with untroubled devotion" (Collect, Ash Wed.); and again, "When you fast, do not show it by gloomy looks" (Gospel, Ash Wed.).

Images of food, however, begin immediately to counterpoint this meaning of fasting; for example, "They all ate the same prophetic food" (Epistle, Septuagesima); "They ate and took their fill" (Communion, Quinquagesima); "Behold, I will send you corn and wine" (Lesson, Ash. Wed.); and then the exquisite poetry of: "Share thy bread with the hungry . . . then sudden as the dawn, the light thou longest for will break upon thee, in a moment thy health shall find fresh vigour; thy righteousness shall lead thee on thy journey, and the brightness of the Lord's presence close thy ranks behind" (Lesson, First Fri., Lent).

Here we see not only images of food, but those of the journey and of light—the light which dawned at Christmas, and shines on into Easter. This light symbolism appears fitfully during Lent, bursts into brilliance with the kindling of the new fire and lighting of the paschal candle at Easter, when we sing, *"Lumen Christi*—the light of Christ"; and is transformed at Pentecost into the flames of the Spirit of Love.

In spite of the wonderful light symbolism of Easter, however, it is even more a time of life issuing from death. Therefore the symbols of food and water which sustain life are more important than those of light. Even during the Lenten period of preparation for Easter, more than twenty distinct references to food are discoverable in the Mass texts. But with Holy Thursday, the day when Christ gave us the bread which was his "flesh for the life of the world"; and continuing to Easter itself and the following forty days, the food symbols are everywhere. Only a few of these references can be traced here, even though a further study of them would be most profitable.

The epistle of Easter Sunday, for example, is all about bread: ourselves as a "new mixture" freed from the old leaven—the yeast of our former self-centered lives; and Christ as the bread of our paschal feast. "Rid yourselves of the leaven which remains over, so that you may be a new mixture. . . . Has not Christ been sacrificed for us, our paschal victim? Let us keep the feast, then, not with the leaven of yesterday, that was all vice and mischief, but with the unleavened bread, with purity and honesty of intent."

Refrains from this epistle echo throughout the Mass, and it concludes with a last reference to food: May "we whose hunger thou hast satisfied with thy Easter sacrament . . . be made one in heart" (Postcomm., Easter Sun.)

Again on Easter Monday we find Peter saying, "We ate and drank in his company after his rising from the dead" (Lesson), and the gospel here is the story (from Luke 24) of the two disciples who, while they walked to the village of Emmaus, were joined by Christ. And they did not recognize him. But "when he sat down at table with them, he took bread, and blessed, and broke it, and offered it to them; whereupon . . . they recognized him."

Christ eats with his disciples, and eats before them, nearly every time he appears. "Have you anything here to eat [he says] So they put before him a piece of roast fish, and a honeycomb; so he ate in their presence and bade them share his meal" (Gospel, Easter Tues.); again on the lake: "They went ashore, and found a charcoal fire . . . with fish and bread cooking on it" (Easter Wed., Gospel). As Ezra Pound, in the poem quoted at the beginning of this section, puts it (in the voice of one of the apostles): "If they think they ha' slain our Goodly Fere / They are fools eternally. / I ha' seen him eat o' the honey-comb / Sin' they nailed him to the tree."

In the Easter Wednesday Mass, this description of the scene at the lake is followed by the offertory verse, "The Lord threw open the doors of heaven and rained down manna for them to eat: the bread of heaven was his gift to them"; and the secret says: "Amid the joys of Easter, Lord, we offer up the sacrifice on which thy Church is wondrously fed and wondrously nourished."

Continually we find such images of food. Finally we come to the three Rogation Days which precede Ascension. These are days dedicated to prayers for the fruitfulness of earth. Following these, the last day of the Easter season, which is Ascension, shows us Christ (in the Lesson) giving his last injunctions to his apostles in the familiar setting of the family meal: "And now he gave them orders, as he shared a meal with them." In the gospel, too, "Jesus appeared to the eleven . . . as they sat at table."

Not only food symbolism, but also images of water and of journeys occur at this time. Christ will journey towards heaven ("I am going up to him who is my Father and your Father"—John 20:17): the apostles are not to leave Jerusalem, not to travel, until the Holy Spirit comes. After that their life-long journeys will begin in earnest: "You are to be my witnesses in Jerusalem and throughout Judea ... and to the ends of the earth" (Lesson, Ascension); they are to "go out all over the world, and preach"; they are to baptize (Gospel, Ascension).

This mention of baptism is explicitly related to the coming of the Holy Spirit which is so soon to occur. "He then laid a charge, by the power of the Holy Spirit, on the apostles ... there is a baptism with the Holy Spirit which you are to receive.... The Holy Spirit will come upon you." He is to be a Spirit of fruitfulness, for as Christ says, "My Father's name [is] glorified, if you yield abundant fruit" (John 15:8).

Easter time, is as we have seen, a time of planting and watering the seed. This seed must first lie in the ground and undergo a certain death. Then it can spring up into new life. The life must grow to maturity and bear fruit. This it does during the next season, which is that of Pentecost.

The days of Pentecost celebrate the coming of the Spirit who warms men into zeal so that they will go out and bear fruit. He makes them branches of the true vine which is Christ, and through this union comes their fruitfulness. As our Lord himself said, "I am the vine, you are its branches; if a man lives on in me, and I in him, then he will yield abundant fruit" (John 15:5). This is only another way of saying that men made fruitful by the coming of the Spirit are to cultivate the fields, and harvest the crops of God's vineyard.

3. *Pentecost*

> The dove descending breaks the air
> With flame of incandescent terror.
>
> T. S. ELIOT [62]

Pentecost season begins with the ten days of preparation immediately following Ascension, and continuing through summer and autumn, ends just before Advent. It is the season of warmth and unity, of love and harvest. As Christmas was the season of light, and Easter the season of life, so Pentecost is the season of love and the fruitfulness of love.

This is a very ancient feast. Scholars believe that what we now call Pentecost was originally a nature festival—a time of rejoicing over the harvest. It was certainly an Old Testament feast. During the old dispensation, the feast of Pentecost came fifty days after the Passover, or Feast of Unleavened Bread. The two days were always looked on as related to one another. And, in like manner, we find that in Christianity, Easter (our passover feast) and Pentecost are linked.

At the Passover, a barley sheaf—that is grain from the fields, not yet made into food for man—was offered to God. Then came a week of weeks (forty-nine days) during which time the grain was reaped. On the fiftieth day, two leavened loaves of wheaten flour were offered to the Lord. This celebration accounts for the fact that so many people were gathered in Jerusalem at the time when the Holy Spirit came. In this providential way, the apostles' message about the good tidings of Christianity was assured of a large audience.

In the New Testament, the Paschal Feast (Passover) was the occasion which Christ chose for the Last Supper. He and his apostles were gathered for its celebration, and at this time he instituted the sacrifice-sacrament of his body and blood in the sign of bread made from grain. Moreover, just as in the old dispensation, the Passover was distinctly linked with Pentecost, so in Christian times, the Paschal sacrifice of Christ led to the gift of the Holy Spirit at Pentecost. As our Lord said, "He who is to befriend you will not come to you unless I . . . go, but if only I make my way there, I will send him to you" (John 16:7).

The historical happening which we commemorate on Pentecost is, then, the coming of the Holy Spirit. We read the story in the *Acts of the Apostles*: When the day of Pentecost came round, while they were all gathered together in unity of purpose, all at once a sound came from heaven like that of a strong wind blowing, and filled the whole house where they were sitting. Then appeared to them what seemed to be tongues of fire, which parted and came to rest on each of them; and they were all filled with the Holy Spirit, and began to speak in strange languages. . . . Each man severally heard them speak in his own language" (Lesson, Pentecost Mass).

Pentecost was, therefore, the occasion on which the outpouring of the Holy Spirit occurred. It became one of the Church's great festivals—the anniversary of the spiritual firstfruits brought about through Christ's sacrifice. Today we look on it and the series of Sundays following it as the time when the fields grow white to the harvest (John 4:35), and the fruits in the Lord's vineyard ripen.

It is, accordingly, the festival time of the maturing of Christ's mystical body here on earth. We, its members, are his harvest. And during this time we discover that the effect of the Spirit on the apostles and on us is unifying and inspiring. We remember that his flame sent the apostles bursting out of the Upper Room, ready to teach Christ in burning words. Because of their zeal, "about three thousand souls were won for the Lord" (Acts 2:41). This was the first reaping. It was a harvest ripened by the Spirit of Love.

The keynote of the season is love. In the Pentecost gospel we read Christ's words about the love and union we are to have with him and the Father: "If a man has any love for me, he will be true to my word; and then he will win my Father's love, and we will both come to him. . . . He who is to befriend you, the Holy Spirit, will . . . make everything plain. . . . If you really loved me, you would be glad to hear that I am on my way to my Father." Then again, in pursuance of this theme, we find on the first Sunday after Pentecost, St. John's discourse which uses the word *love* twenty-three times in fourteen verses. The keynote is that "love resides, not in our showing any love for God, but in his showing love for us first."

In this season of unity and culmination, all the four elements of earth, air, fire, and water, with their symbolic meanings appear. The imagery of water is carried over from Easter, for this too is a time for baptisms. And air is here, as breath and as wind—the wind of the Spirit who is the breathing forth of love between the Father and the Word. This is the wind whose effect is to shape man's breath into speech—a gift of tongues which will speak words. And the wind of the Spirit will carry these words to all parts of the world.

Christ himself pointed up the connection between the wind and the Spirit, long before Pentecost. We have heard the words before: "Do not be surprised . . . at my telling thee, You must be born anew. The wind breathes where it will, and thou canst hear the sound of it, but knowest nothing of the way it came or the way it goes; so it is, when a man is born by the breath of the Spirit" (John 3:7-8).

This connection, which Christ has called to our attention, is actualized by the coming of the Holy Spirit: "While they were all gathered . . . all at once a sound came from heaven like that of a strong wind blowing" (Acts 2:1-2). This breath of the Spirit, as it were, blows the apostles out of their quiet Upper Room, to the four corners of the world. As Paul Claudel, the modern French poet once put it:

> There is a Wind, I mean the Spirit, which is sweeping nations with a broom.
> When you have it unchained, it sets all the human landscape a-moving.
> Ideas from one end of the world to the other are catching fire like stubble.[63]

The wind comes, and this is one element. But the Spirit appears under the form of another of the elements. He comes in tongue of fire: "Then appeared . . . tongues of fire . . . and they were filled with the Holy Spirit, and began to speak in strange languages" (Acts 2:3-4). The picture appears as if the apostles were made into living torches (the fire "came to rest on each of them"); the flame of the Spirit settled on every one. And they left their retreat fired with enthusiasm. Like torches, they not only gave light, but they also set aflame everything they touched.

To send out men into the world—apostles of the Word of God—this is the intent of the Holy Ghost. And for this purpose, he invests these men not only with zeal, necessary as that is, but also with tact. Tact means the ability to talk every man's language, to take each one as he is and reach him on his own terms. And this is what we find happening here at-Pentecost—"How is it that each of us hears them talking his own native tongue? . . . Each has been hearing them tell of God's wonders in his own language" (Acts 2:8-12). Such is one reason that the flame appeared as tongues.

Finally, the fourth element, earth and its fruitfulness, is the most important of all during this season of Pentecost. We think back to the time of Lent for the beginning of the long fruition. At that time we "went and wept, casting [our] seeds" (Ps. 125:6, Douay) in hopes of a spiritual harvesting. Or rather, we, like seeds ourselves, were cast into the ground to die along with Christ.

But at Easter time the warmth of joy caused the seed to break out of the dark ground. Gradually it grew and ripened, and then when the wind of the Spirit blew at last, it was ready for harvesting. Then "was our mouth filled with gladness: and our tongue with joy. [And we said] The Lord hath done great things for us: we are become joyful. [Now we know] they that sow in tears shall reap in joy. . . . Coming they shall come with joyfulness, carrying their sheaves" (Ps. 125:2-7, Douay).

Such is the growth of the spiritual life, and the development of the Pentecostal fruitfulness. This harvest theme suits the natural season (at least in the northern hemisphere), because summer and fall are times of harvest. The crop in the supernatural world is to be a heavenly one. It is made of the souls which Christ was seeing when he said, "And look at the fields, they are white with a promise of harvest already" (John 4:35). This maturation comes about through union with Christ the vine, as we have said. "I am the vine," he tells us, "you are its branches; if a man lives on in me, and I in him, then he will yield abundant fruit" (John 15:5).

This union with Christ which issues in fruitfulness is the proper work of the Spirit of Love, for love is a unifying force, and fruitfulness is a result of union. From this union springs our zeal to further the growth of the kingdom of God.

This is the work of the apostle, whether he lived in the first century in Palestine, or lives now in the twentieth century in America. Our Lord used another metaphor for this same idea when he told Peter and the others that he would make them "fishers of men" (Mark 1:17). This, then, is the harvest—a multitude of souls gathered into the heavenly fold praising God and rejoicing together for all eternity.

Hopkins' poem, "The Starlight Night," describes the final harvest. He says that the night sky with its bright stars is a wall—the wall of a barn. And within that barn the crops, the fruits of God's harvesting (namely, Christ and his mother, and all the saints) are stored:

> These [stars and skies] are indeed the barn; withindoors house
> The shocks. This piece-bright paling shuts the spouse
> Christ home, Christ and his mother and all his hallows.[64]

With these meanings in mind, let us gather a few of the harvest and fruitfulness references from the Masses of the Pentecost season. First, there is the refrain which begins on Pentecost Sunday and recurs frequently. It reminds us once more of the Spirit in Genesis brooding over chaos, causing it to become fruitful: "Send forth thy Spirit, and there will be fresh creation; thou wilt repeople the earth. . . . Come, Holy Spirit, fill the hearts of thy faithful and kindle in them the fire of thy love."

Then come such images as: "May our souls grow fertile under the dew he [the Spirit] sheds upon them" (Postcomm., Pentecost Sun.); "Full ears of wheat are the nourishment he gives them, alleluia, and honey dripping from the rock to their hearts' content" (Introit, Pent. Mon.). Again we find: "Now the threshing-floor shall be piled with wheat, and the presses overflow with wine and oil" (Lesson, Pent. Fri.); "You must bring sheaves of corn, the firstfruits of your crop, to the priest, and he . . . will consecrate each sheaf" (Lesson 2, Pent. Sat.). Finally the last one we shall show here is particularly beautiful: "Rain will fall on you when rain it should; the land will yield its increase, and the trees will be bowed with fruit, threshing not done with by vintage time, or vintage by seed-time" (Lesson 4, Pent. Sat.).

Many such symbols and images of growth, fruit, and harvest occur during the long series of Sundays after Pentecost. Sometimes we find several of them in a single Mass, then again they will disappear for a week or even two. But their appearance is frequent enough to show that the main theme of the time is a love and unity brought about by the Holy Spirit in order that souls may bear fruit.

This is the longest season of the year, and sometimes it may seem monotonous. The fact is, that here as in nature, planting is swift and filled with hard work and varied happenings, but ripening time for crops is slow—leisured and undisturbed.

All three seasons, as was said earlier, center around Christ. This is obvious in the case of Christmas and Easter. In the former season we commemorate the birth of Christ and his hidden years at home. During the latter, we think how he accomplished his mission, especially his main task of dying and rising again for our salvation.

But what about Pentecost. Is not this the season of the Holy Spirit? Clearly, it is. But along with our awareness of the Third Person, we also celebrate a life of Christ. Now, however, it is no longer the historical life of Christ, which happened at a certain time, and in the specific country of Palestine. Then he lived and grew in historical time, confined to a certain place and era. These historical mysteries are the ones we celebrate in the first two seasons. In the third we do commemorate the Holy Spirit. But he is also the Spirit of Christ. Therefore we see Christ—the Mystical Christ—live and work and grow.

This is what Cardinal Suhard meant, when in the phrase we have quoted before, he said, "Christ must become incarnate in each generation." It is this incarnation which we see in process through the work of the Holy Spirit during our days and in our country. Christ is, here and now, in us his members, growing and working and harvesting souls for the glory of his Father.

The last Sunday of the year, which is the last Sunday after Pentecost, bears the theme of the world's end. At this time the harvest will really be complete, for all the tribes and peoples and nations will rise and come together. They will come from the sea, as Sister Maris Stella describes the scene:

> From the deep sea wrack
> from the green light under the sea
> from the coral caves men will come back

They will also come from every place on earth—these men of every age:

> on mountain tops where
> dropped from the air
> or hurled
> against the world . . .
> among the old
> rock-frost above the tree-line

Into them all, God will breathe life as he did at the first creation, and then the whole Christ will be complete to the last member:

> they will rise up with the divine
> breath breathed into them again
> as on the first of men
> Adam, newly conceived of clay
> on the sixth day God breathed
> even somewhere Adam will rise [65]

This culmination is described in the Apocalypse: "He showed me, too, a river, whose waters give life; it flows clear as crystal, from the throne of God, from the throne of the Lamb. On either side of the river . . . grows the tree that gives life, bearing its fruit twelve-fold, one yield for each month. . . . God's throne (which is the Lamb's throne) will be there with his servants to worship him, and to see his face. . . . There will be no more night, no more need of light from lamp or sun; the Lord God will shed his light on them" (Apoc. 22:1-5).

This is the completion, the harvest of which all natural harvests are foreshadowings. In St. John's glowing words all things are brought together, mankind and God, the river, the fruit of the earth and the harvest of heaven—all lighted by the brightness of the Lord God.

Thus finally the harvest will be gathered in, and the last circles of recurring Masses, sacramental helps to men's lives, days blessed by the praying of the Hours, and years consecrated by the holy seasons will be complete.

And in another sense, there will be no more circles. Recurrence and return as we know them will be no more. The movement of time will be transfigured into the utter and intense activity of the vision of God which suffers no change: perfect actualization and complete quietude

We might describe all this in the lovely lines of Eliot which fuse a phrase from Julian of Norwich with an image from Dante:

> ... all shall be well and
> All manner of thing shall be well
> When the tongues of flame are in-folded
> Into the crowned knot of fire
> And the fire and the rose are one.[66]

As we finish our leisured and inclusive view of the world of worship, let us look one last time at some of the things we have discovered. The whole book has been an analysis and a synthesis. We have considered many separate designs, themes and symbols, but only in order to see them more clearly when they are put back in their places. Our analysis has been made only that the final synthesis might embrace more of reality.

While we have looked with intent and quiet gaze, we have seen that all things are given dignity because they share in the worship of God. We have rejoiced because on this earth even our vision of the glory of God comes to us through concrete materialities: through the humanity of Christ the center of all, and through our familiar elements of earth, air, fire, and water. We have been gladdened because these things enrich our worship of God, and because the natural world and all the things made by man are in their turn illumined by the liturgy.

Because the liturgy is the greatest unifying force in the world, therefore, as St. Paul says, "Grace made manifold in many lives may increase the sum of gratitude which is offered to God's glory" (II Cor. 4:15). Living thus in the liturgy's spirit of joyous praise, we can hasten the final transfiguration of ourselves and our world. When this is complete we will need no more epiphanies of art—there will be no more art. The last and final epiphany will be ours. And there will be God.

APPENDIX I

Of the Illustrations

I. *They Have No Wine:* "There was a wedding feast at Cana, in Galilee; and Jesus' mother was there. Jesus himself . . . had also been invited. . . . Here the supply of wine failed; whereupon Jesus' mother said to him, They have no wine left" (John 2:1-3).

II. *Consider the Lilies:* "See how the lilies grow; they do not toil, or spin, and yet I tell you that even Solomon in all his glory was not arrayed as one of these" (Luke 12:27).

III. *I Know Mine:* "I am the good shepherd. The good shepherd lays down his life for his sheep" (John 10:11-12).

IV. *Give Me the Living Water:* "How is it that thou, who art a Jew, dost ask of me, a Samaritan, to give thee drink? . . . Jesus answered her, if thou knewest what it is God gives, and who this is that is saying to thee, Give me drink, it would have been for thee to ask him instead, and he would have given thee living water" (John 4:10).

V. *I Am Not Worthy:* "Lord, he said; I am not worthy to receive thee under my roof. . . . My servant will be healed if thou wilt only speak a word of command" (Matt. 8:8).

VI. "*If only I am lifted up* from the earth, I will attract all men to myself" (John 12:31).

VII. *Mass Symbol.* The center figure pictures the movement of the Mass. Around the large circle, the small circles picture the same movement: 1) folded hands, we speak to God; 2) gospel book; he speaks to us; 3) we give fruits of the earth; 4) God makes Calvary present, and we offer Christ's sacrifice; 5) God gives us Christ in the Eucharist; 6) we speak to God and he blesses us—hand raised in blessing; 7) we carry out the lamp of grace to light the world.

VIII. *Sacraments.* Christ at center, rays radiate out to us from him. Baptism, candle and white robe; confirmation, Holy Spirit in form of dove; Eucharist, host and chalice; penance, keys for binding and loosing; last anointing, olive branch and vessel; holy orders, priestly vestments and candle of fealty; matrimony, Chi-Rho, sign for Christ, uniting two rings.

IX. *Office.* Christ at center in form of Chi-Rho. Rays of our praise go inward to him. Symbols of night (Matins); dawn (Lauds); day's work (Prime); Holy Spirit (Terce); Christ on cross (Sext); empty cross and hint of resurrection (None); censer for evening sacrifice of praise (Vespers); Chi-Rho for Christ who is Son of Mary (*M*), like candle watching our rest (Compline).

X. *Year.* Triangle and circle, symbols for unity and trinity of God. Key words of seasons: *Gloria, Alleluia, Veni.* Key feasts (Christmas, Easter, Pentecost) at corners of triangle. Around circle: crib at top, Christmas; candle for Presentation; nails and crown, Good Friday; paschal candle, Easter; Lower center, pierced feet of Christ in his Ascension; dove for Pentecost; lily for Mary's Assumption, comes in summer—days after Pent., ripening and harvest time; keys for end of world, opening of gates, storing of harvest.

APPENDIX II

Of the Authors Quoted

1. Dom Ildefons Herwegen, *The Art Principle of the Liturgy* (Collegeville, Minnesota: The Liturgical Press, 1931), pp. 15-16.

2. T. S. Eliot, "Burnt Norton," *The Complete Poetry and Plays* (New York: Harcourt, Brace and Company, 1952), p. 121. This edition will be referred to as *Complete Poems*.

3. I first heard this phrase used in lectures at Catholic University of America by Rev. Godfrey Diekmann, O.S.B.

4. On this page and the next one I have used some material from my article, "Adventures in Looking," which appeared in *Today*, June 1955.

5. Julian, Anchoress at Norwich, A.D. 1373, *Revelations of Divine Love*, edited by Grace Warrack (London: Methuen and Co., Ltd. 1949), p. liii.

6. Gerard Manley Hopkins, "The Wreck of the Deutschland," *The Poems of Gerard Manley Hopkins* (New York: Oxford University Press, 1948), p. 66. This edition will be referred to as *Poems*.

7. Epigraph, Christopher Fry, quoted by Derek Stanford in *Christopher Fry* (New York: Longmans, Green and Co., 1954), p. 25. This quotation is used again later.

8. Hopkins, "The Caged Skylark," *Poems*, p. 75.

9. Carron Vincent, "tight-rope," prize-winning poem as yet unpublished. Used with permission of the author.

10. Scriptural quotations are from *The Old Testament* and *The New Testament*, translated by Msgr. Ronald Knox (New York: Sheed and Ward, 1950, and 1954 respectively), except where otherwise specified.

11. Alice Meynell, "'I Am the Way,'" *The Poems of Alice Meynell* (London: Oxford University Press, 1941), p. 80.

12. All quotations of Mass texts are from *The Missal in Latin and English* (New York: Sheed and Ward, 1949).

13. T. S. Eliot, "La Figlia Che Piange," *Complete Poems*, p. 20.

14. John Donne, "Holy Sonnets, 10," *The Poems of John Donne*, edited by Sir Herbert Grierson (New York: Oxford University Press, 1951), p. 297.

15. Dante Alighieri, *The Divine Comedy*, translated by H. R. Huse (New York: Rinehart and Co., Inc., 1954), all quotations are from this edition.

16. Christopher Fry, *The Firstborn* (New York: Oxford University Press, 1950), p. 29.

17. Epigraph, Christopher Fry, *The Boy with a Cart* (New York: Oxford University Press, 1951), pp. 1, 2.

18. Epigraph, Henry Vaughan, "The World," *Silex Scintillans* (London: Geo. Bell and Sons, 1890), p. 126.

19. Fry, *Boy with a Cart*, p. 4.

20. Eliot, "Burnt Norton," *Complete Poems*, p. 119.

21. Vaughan, *loc. cit.*

22. Donne, "A Valediction: Forbidding Mourning," *op. cit.*, p. 44.

23. Fry, *Boy with a Cart*, p. 40.

24. Epigraph, Matthias Joseph Scheeben, *The Mysteries of Christianity*, translated by Cyril Vollert, S. J. (St. Louis: B. Herder Book Co., 1947), p. 654.

25. Herwegen, *op. cit.*, p. 16.

26. Dylan Thomas, "Fern Hill," *The Collected Poetry of Dylan Thomas* (New York: New Directions, 1953), p. 178. This edition will be referred to as *Collected Poems*. Some of the ideas here are from my article on Dylan Thomas which appeared in *The Explicator*, October 1955.

27. Herwegen, *loc. cit.*

APPENDICES

28. Archbishop Alban Goodier, S. J., *The Public Life of Our Lord Jesus Christ* (New York: P. J. Kenedy and Sons, 1944), vol. 2.

29. Charles Péguy, *God Speaks*, translated by Julian Green (New York: Pantheon Books, Inc., 1945), pp. 50-51.

30. Scheeben, *op. cit.*, p. 562.

31. Ronald Knox, *Holy Week* (New York: Sheed and Ward, 1951), p. 328.

32. *Ibid.*, p. 334.

33. Sheed and Ward Missal, "The Order of Blessing Holy Water," pp. 257*–259*.

34. Epigraph, Dylan Thomas, "Poem on His Birthday," *Collected Poems*, pp. 192-3.

35. Hopkins, "The Blessed Virgin Compared to the Air We Breathe," *Poems*, p. 100.

36. *Ibid.*, "God's Grandeur," p. 70.

37. Eliot, "The Waste Land," and "Murder in the Cathedral," *Complete Poems*, pp. 37 and 176 respectively.

38. Suzanne Langer, *Feeling and Form* (New York: Charles Scribner's Sons, 1953), p. 28.

39. Karl Jung, *Integration of Personality*, translated by Stanley Dell (New York: Farrar and Rinehart, Inc., 1939), p. 89.

40. Epigraph, Julian of Norwich, *op. cit.*, p. 26.

41. Eunice Tietjens, "The Most-Sacred Mountain," *New Voices*, edited by Marguerite Wilkinson (New York: Macmillan Co., 1929), p. 80.

42. Romano Guardini, *The Spirit of the Liturgy* (London: Sheed and Ward, 1930), p. 125.

43. Louis Bouyer, *Liturgical Piety* (Notre Dame, Ind.: University of Notre Dame Press, 1954), p. 131.

44. Rev. Godfrey Diekmann suggests this idea in *Mass Symbols* (Collegeville, Minn.: The Liturgical Press, 1947), p. 37.

45. Epigraph, Dylan Thomas, *Collected Poems*, p. 185.

46. Abbot Columba Marmion, *A Master of the Spiritual Life* (St. Louis: B. Herder Co., 1949), p. 136.

47. Dylan Thomas, *Quite Early One Morning* (New York: New Directions, 1954), p. 106.

48. These blessings are from *Roman Ritual: The Blessings*, translated by Rev. Philip T. Weller (Milwaukee: The Bruce Publishing Co., 1945), vol. 3.

49. The quotations from the texts of the sacraments are from: *The Gift of Life* (baptism), *The Seal of the Spirit* (confirmation), *Marriage in Christ, God's Healing* (extreme unction), (Collegeville, Minn.: The Liturgical Press). Those from holy orders: *The Rite of Ordination* (Westminster, Maryland: The Newman Bookshop, 1944).

50. Eliot, "The Journey of the Magi," *Complete Poems*, p. 68.

51. Epigraph, Abbot Columba Marmion, O.S.B., *Christ the Ideal of the Monk* (St. Louis: B. Herder Co., 1925), pp. 291, 322, 295.

52. *The Roman Breviary in English* (New York: Benziger Brothers, Inc., 1941). Quotations from the text of the office are from this breviary. This includes scriptural quotations in this chapter.

53. Epigraph, Eliot, "Murder in the Cathedral," *Complete Poems*, p. 221.

54. Dylan Thomas, "Fern Hill," *Collected Poems*, p. 178.

55. Hopkins, "The Wreck of the Deutschland," *Poems*, p. 67.

56. Epigraph, Eliot, "Ash Wednesday," *Complete Poems*, p. 65.

57. Thomas Merton, "The Candlemas Procession," *A Man in a Divided Sea* (New York: New Directions, 1946), p. 56.

58. Epigraph, Ezra Pound, "Ballad of the Goodly Fere," (New York: New Directions, 1949), p. 16.

59. Romano Guardini, *The Lord* (Chicago: Henry Regnery Co., 1954), p. 236.

60. John Milton, *Paradise Lost*, Book One, lines 19-23.

61. Hopkins, "God's Grandeur," *Poems*, p. 70.

62. Epigraph, Eliot, "Little Gidding," *Complete Poems*, p. 143.

63. Paul Claudel, *The Satin Slipper* (New York: Sheed and Ward, n.d.), p. vi.

64. Hopkins, "The Starlight Night," *Poems*, pp. 70-71.

65. Sister Maris Stella, C.S.J., "Resurrection," *Frost for St. Brigid* (New York: Sheed and Ward, 1949), p. 3.

66. Eliot, "Little Gidding," *Complete Poems*, p. 145.

CPSIA information can be obtained
at www.ICGtesting.com
Printed in the USA
LVHW050945210221
679536LV00034B/1074